AN ENGLISH SELF-STUDY SUPPLEMENT TO LEVEND NEDERLANDS

An audiovisual Dutch language
course for foreigners
3rd edition

Dr. Jan H. Hulstijn

Lecturer in Dutch as a Second Language
Free University of Amsterdam

Dr. Michael Hannay

Lecturer in Modern English
Free University of Amsterdam

VU Uitgeverij
Amsterdam 1987

LEVEND NEDERLANDS

Een audio-visuele cursus Nederlands voor buitenlanders

De cursus Levend Nederlands bestaat uit:

Leerboek
Oefenmateriaal
An English Self-Study Supplement
Suplemento para el estudio autodidactico
Supplément français pour l'autodidacte
Aanvullende woordenlijst
Filmstrips
Tape Recordings
Cassettes

CIP-GEGEVENS KONINKLIJKE BIBLIOTHEEK, DEN HAAG

Hulstijn, Jan H.

An English self-study supplement to Levend Nederlands :
an audiovisual Dutch language course for foreigners /
Jan H. Hulstijn, Michael Hannay. - Amsterdam : VU Uitgeverij
Met index.
ISBN 90-6256-459-3
SISO * 838.5 UDC 372.880.393 NUGI 942
Trefw.: Nederlandse taal voor buitenlanders.

VU Uitgeverij is een imprint van:
VU Boekhandel/Uitgeverij b.v.
De Boelelaan 1105
1081 HV Amsterdam

1e druk (1981) isbn 90-6256-381-3
2e druk (1985) isbn 90-6256-337-6
3e druk (1987) isbn 90-6256-459-3 nugi 942

© VU Boekhandel/Uitgeverij b.v., Amsterdam, 1987.

CONTENTS

FOREWORD

This supplement constitutes a major reworking of *Levend Nederlands: Supplement for the Self-instructional Student.* It differs from the original work in a number of important respects. In the first instance we have endeavoured to make this supplement a more handy and presentable workbook for the student, to which end a printed edition has been produced, in a new format, a more fluid and coherent style, and with a substantial reference and index system.

Equally important, however, is the undertaking of a complete revision of the contents. A number of grammar sections have been substantially rewritten in the light of experiences gained in the last three years in the teaching of Dutch as a second language at the Free University. In many cases numerous examples have also been added to facilitate the understanding of Dutch constructions, particularly in the case of sentence adverbials, the command of which so much depends on acquiring a feeling for the word. Moreover, changes in attitudes in the Dutch-speaking area in recent years, particularly among younger people, have provoked us to offer a much fuller treatment of, for instance, forms of greeting and address. Despite this large-scale revision, no significant modifications have, however, been made in the ordering per lesson of grammar points etc., since the dialogues and the exercises in the course book remain unchanged.

We are much indebted to Alice van Kalsbeek, whose energy and conscientiousness contributed so much to the composing of the first supplement, which formed the essential basis for the present work. Finally we owe our gratitude to Roel Vismans, who with diligence and devotion typed the manuscript.

J.H.H. Free University of Amsterdam
M.H. November 1980

INTRODUCTION

1 THE AIM OF THE COURSE

This guide for the self-study student is a supplement to *Levend Nederlands, een audiovisuele cursus Nederlands voor buitenlanders* (Cambridge University Press, 1975, Revised Edition 1984). *Levend Nederlands* is a course aimed at providing practice in understanding and producing educated, spoken Dutch. This supplement was in the first instance designed for the great number of foreigners who are not in a position to attend classes.

An advantage of self-study is that you can study at your own pace. You are advised to study regularly and not for too long at a time. It is, for example, better to work 2 hours every day than 5 or 6 hours once a week.

We advise you to adhere to the order of the material and to the procedure suggested in this guide. It will not be necessary to consult the introduction on page X/XI of the course book; all instructions can be found in the present Introduction.

In the instructions in section 3 of this Introduction we assume the use of tapes which contain dialogues at normal speed, followed by dialogues and exercises with pauses in between utterances, whereas commercial tapes do not contain pauses.

2 THE MATERIAL

2.1 The material making up this course consists of:
1. the course book *Levend Nederlands, een audiovisuele cursus Nederlands voor buitenlanders* (Cambridge University Press, Revised Edition 1984)
2. tapes (cassettes)
3. this English Supplement
4. the book of exercises entitled *Oefenmateriaal behorend bij Levend Nederlands.* It is not necessary for the self-study student to make use of this book.

The course consists of 24 lessons. Lesson 1 deals with phonetics and spelling. Lessons 2–24 each consist of:
- *het gesprek*/the dialogue (in the course book; on the tape)
- *aanvullende fonetiek*/supplementary phonetics (in the course book; on the tape)
- *samenvatting van de dialoog*/summary of the dialogue (in the course book; on the tape)
- *oefeningen*/exercises (in the course book; on the tape)
- *aanvullende woordenlijst*/supplementary glossary (in the course book)
- *vragen over het gesprek*/questions concerning the dialogue (in the course book)
- *conversatie*/conversation (in the course book)
- *huiswerk*/homework (in the course book)

This supplement contains for each lesson a summary of the dialogue, a set of grammar notes and a section entitled 'further remarks'.

2.2 SCHEMATIC SURVEY OF THE MATERIAL

The following schematic survey of the material shows what kinds of material, exercises etc. make up one lesson.

The various blocks should be studied in the right order. Blocks **A, D, E** are the most important parts of the lesson; they must be studied in order to proceed to the next lesson. **B, C, F** are less important: it is up to you to study them or leave them out. **G** is useful if you have a teacher in that it can provide a basis for conversation.

SURVEY OF THE MATERIAL MAKING UP ONE LESSON

	I Tapes	II Course book	III Supplement
A			Summary of the dialogue
	Gesprek – fast version – slow version	*Gesprek* – text – pictures	
B	*Aanvullende fonetiek*	*Aanvullende fonetiek*	
C	*Samenvatting*	*Samenvatting*	
D			Grammar Further remarks
E	*Oefeningen*	*Oefeningen*	
F		*Aanvullende woordenlijst*	
G		*Vragen over het gesprek* *Conversatie* *Huiswerk*	

3   HOW TO WORK WITH THE SEPARATE PARTS OF THE COURSE

Below are detailed instructions for studying a lesson. Of course several methods are possible and the choice between them is, ultimately, a personal one. For the present, however, it is better to adhere to the instructions given below. You are advised to defer the study of lesson 1 until you have studied some of the following lessons. Separate instructions for lesson 1 are to be found in section 3.9 below.

INTRODUCTION

3.1 DIALOGUE

The dialogue forms the basis of each unit. It normally contains 70–72 lines, each being illustrated by a picture. When working with the dialogue, you should proceed as follows:

1. Read the summary of the dialogue in the Supplement. This gives an outline of the situation in which the dialogue takes place, and also mentions the grammatical teaching points covered in the lesson.
2. Listen to the first version of the dialogue on the tape and look at the pictures in the book. In this version, the dialogue is so fast that it is not possible to read the text while listening. This first run-through is only to give an understanding of the dialogue as a whole.
3. The second reading of the dialogue on the tape is a slow version. First look at the picture and the text in the course book, then switch on the tape recorder. After the first sentence comes a short pause, during which you must try to repeat the sentence. If the pause is not long enough, you must stop the tape. Work through the whole dialogue in this manner. Once you have done this, stop the tape and rewind to the beginning of the slow version in order to listen to your own voice or to repeat the sentences once again. It is important here that you try to notice the often considerable differences between what you hear on the tape and the written text in the book: make careful comparisons of pronunciation and spelling. You can go through this stage as often as you think useful.

When you have familiarised yourself with the dialogue in this way, you should be able to repeat the sentences from the tape correctly without reading the text simultaneously. Cover the text of the dialogue with a piece of paper, listen to the sentence on the tape, repeat this sentence and then uncover the same sentence in the text to check whether you have succeeded in understanding and repeating all the words correctly.

3.2 GRAMMAR AND FURTHER REMARKS

4. After having gone through the dialogue you proceed to the 'Grammar' section in the Supplement. This survey treats the grammatical teaching points covered in the dialogue. The numbers between round brackets indicate the lines in the dialogue, whereby '1.' stands for 'line'. References to particular exercises can be found on the right hand side of the page at the beginning of the relevant grammar notes. You can check if you have understood the grammatical rules by looking at the exercises in the course book.
5. Read the dialogue line by line and see if you really understand every word. Look up new words in the dictionary. A number of fixed expressions and further information on vocabulary and aspects of meaning are found (in the order in which they occur in the dialogue) in the 'Further remarks' section in this Supplement.
6. At this stage the dialogue should not present any difficulties to you any more. Listen to the slow version of the dialogue once again. You should now be capable of understanding and repeating all sentences without looking at the text.

3.3   SUPPLEMENTARY PHONETICS

Following the slow version of the dialogue, there are a number of instructions on the tape concerning exceptional cases of spelling and pronunciation. The voice on the tape usually says:

'*Let op de uitspraak van . . .*' ('pay attention to the pronunciation of . . .')

'*Herhaal . . .*' ('repeat')

Then you may repeat what is said on the tape. Carefully compare the pronunciation with the spelling (see the text in the course book) and your pronunciation with the voice on the tape.

3.4   THE EXERCISES

The exercises provide practice in forming Dutch sentences based on patterns which have been introduced in the dialogue and which are explicated in the 'Grammar' sections. We distinguish two kinds of exercises: stimulus - response exercises and substitution exercises.

3.4.1. Stimulus - response exercises

In these drills you are required to change the structure of sentences. You will first hear an example of the original sentence ('stimulus') and the response required ('stimulus' and 'response' are often shortened to 'S' and 'R'). E.g.

bent u student? (S)	are you a student?
ja, ik ben student (R)	yes, I'm a student

Then you hear other sentences (S) parallel to the stimulus, to which you must give the proper response yourself. It is necessary to decide what happened to the original S of the example in order to be able to produce the same kind of response as the example R.

On the tape every S is followed by a pause for you to formulate your R. If you find the pause too short, stop the tape after S, give yourself some extra seconds to think, and then switch on the tape and record your response. After your response comes a model response as a guide to the correctness of your response. Then there is another pause in which the response can be spoken again. This activity continues to the end of the drill.

To summarise, each exercise item consists of:
1. stimulus from the tape
2. pause for you to respond
3. correct response from the tape
4. pause for you to repeat the correct response

3.4.2 Substitution exercises

With these exercises you first hear a sentence and then a word or word group. E.g.

ik werk in Amsterdam	*woon*

You have to make a new sentence by replacing a part of the original sentence by the word or word group that follows it. The pattern of the sentence remains the same; only a part of the

INTRODUCTION

sentence is replaced. This need not always be the same constituent. You have to know which part of the sentence is to be replaced. In the example above it is the conjugated form of the verb: *werk → woon.* The new sentence is:

ik woon in Amsterdam

The correct sentence can be heard on the tape. It is followed by a pause during which you can repeat it. This correct sentence serves as a basis for the next substitution item:

ik woon in Amsterdam   *hij*
hij woont in Amsterdam
etc.

3.4.3 If an exercise is too hard for you because you cannot understand the stimulus sentence or you do not know how to make the proper response, you can glance through the exercises in the course book. However, the last time you do an exercise you should be able to do it without the help of the written text. Just as with the dialogue, you may cover the text with a piece of paper and only uncover the line for checking after you have tried to do the item in question without the help of the written text. If or when you find an exercise easy (both comprehension and production), you might pay special attention to intonation and pronunciation.

3.5. *SAMENVATTING* (you can find this on the tape after 'Supplementary phonetics')
Some suggestions for how to use the *samenvatting:*

1. You can **listen** to the *samenvatting.* Since it deals with a situation you are familiar with, there should be no problem about the meaning of the dialogue as a whole.
2. It may be **read** through quickly, again in order to get some idea as to what the dialogue is about.
3. The *samenvatting* may be used as a **dictation passage.** Listen to the tape and try to write down what you hear. If you cannot write down a full sentence at one time, stop the tape every now and then. Compare your notes with the text in the course book.

3.6. *AANVULLENDE WOORDENLIJST*

The *aanvullende woordenlijst* is a list of words used in connection with topics which occur in the dialogue. They are followed by a story. You may look up the words in your dictionary in order to enlarge your basic vocabulary.

3.7 *VRAGEN OVER HET GESPREK* AND *CONVERSATIE*

How you deal with the questions depends on whether you have a teacher or not. If you do not have a teacher, try to answer them for yourself. If you do have a teacher, the questions may help you to prepare for the conversation which you will have with him. Another possibility is to write down the answers and have your teacher correct them.

6

3.8 *HUISWERK*

If you have no teacher you should correct your homework yourself with the help of the answers on page 220–222 of the course book. You may also find a native speaker who is willing to correct your work for you. In that case, it is also possible to answer the 'open questions'. It is always very useful to do the homework as a test to find out whether you have mastered the grammar or not.

3.9 LESSON 1

It is advisable to start your studies with lesson 2 and to do lesson 1, if at all, after you have covered a number of the other lessons.

In this lesson you are required to distinguish the pronunciation of groups of words in short sentences which clearly differ in meaning but differ only in one sound (e.g. *een pit, een pet, een put*). There is a picture corresponding with each word. You have to determine which word on the tape corresponds with which picture and then you have to pronounce the words after each other, concentrating on the differences in sound. In this way you learn simultaneously how to read and spell the written words (so no pen and paper are necessary).

There are 3 voices on the tape. The first (the 'commentator') gives information and instructions; the second (the 'model speaker') says the words that you have to repeat and the questions you have to answer; the third (the 'exemplary student') only occurs in the beginning to demonstrate what you have to do.

There are also 2 signals: a high tone meaning 'look at the next picture', and a low tone meaning 'no picture', in which case you should look up from the book and listen to the commentator.

LESSON 2

1. SUMMARY OF THE DIALOGUE

On the boat from England to Holland Kees Bergsma, a student from Amsterdam, meets an English journalist, John King, who also lives in Amsterdam and speaks good Dutch.

Pay attention to: – the combination $\frac{ik}{u}$ + *persoonsvorm*

           – the order of the various words and groups in the sentences

N.B. The *persoonsvorm* (henceforth PV) is the conjugated form of the verb (i.e. the finite form).

The words in bold face in the following examples are all PVs:

I **work**
He **works**
I **worked**
I **am** working
I **have** worked

TRANSLATION OF THE DIALOGUE

K. I live in Amsterdam.
J. Are you a student?
K. Yes, I'm a student.   (3)
  I study English.
J. So, you study English, do you?
  Well, that's my native language.   (6)
K. Your language?
  You're not Dutch, then?
J. No, I'm English.   (9)
K. Your Dutch is very good, Sir.
J. Thank you.
  My mother is Dutch.   (12)
K. Oh, isn't your mother English?
J. No, my mother is Dutch
  and my father is English.   (15)
  You're Dutch, aren't you?
K. Yes, I'm Dutch.
  Are you a student as well?   (18)
J. No, I'm a journalist.
K. Do you work in Holland?
J. Yes, I work in Amsterdam.   (21)
K. Do you live in Amsterdam as well?
J. Yes, in the Leidsestraat.
K. I live on the Hoofdweg.   (24)
  Why don't you drop by some time?
J. What did you say?

K. Why don't you drop by some time? (27)
J. Yes, I'd like to.
K. I'm Kees Bersma.
My address is Hoofdweg 2, Amsterdam. (30)
J. Thank you very much, Mr Bergsma.
My name is John King.
I'll drop by soon.

2. GRAMMAR

2.1 PRONOUNS
2.1.1 Personal pronouns 1st and 2nd singular
E. 1-9, 14

The sentences in the dialogue of this lesson all consist of a subject, a PV and a remaining constituent. e.g.

ik woon in Amsterdam (line 1)

One of the categories that may function as subject is the personal pronoun. In this lesson we deal with the personal pronouns of the 1st and 2nd person singular in the subject form. The personal pronoun takes the subject form if it operates as subject of the sentence. The 1st person singular pronoun is *ik*. The 2nd person singular pronoun is in certain cases *u* (e.g. in formal situations).
In this lesson John and Kees say *u* to each other because they have never met before.

bent u dan geen Nederlander? (1.8) you're not Dutch, then?
u bent Nederlander, hè? (1.16) you're Dutch, aren't you?

2.1.2 Possessive pronouns of the 1st and 2nd person singular
E. 12, 13

Each personal pronoun has a corresponding possessive pronoun. For *ik* and *u* these are *m'n* (usually spelt *mijn*) and *uw* respectively:

	personal pronoun	possessive pronoun
1st person singular	*ik*	*mijn*
2nd person singular (formal)	*u*	*uw*

ik ben Kees Bergsma (1.29) I am Kees Bergsma
mijn naam is Kees Bergsma my name is Kees Bergsma
u bent John King you are John King
uw naam is John King your name is John King

LESSON 2

2.2 VERBS

2.2.1 The PV of the 1st, 2nd and 3rd person singular
E. 3, 4, 6–8, 10

In the sentence *ik woon in Amsterdam*, *woon* is the PV of the 1st person singular. In the present tense this PV is usually identical with the stem of the verb:

ik woon   I live
ik studeer   I study

The stem of the verb is the form to which the inflectional endings are attached. The stem of Dutch verbs is to be found by removing the ending *-n* or *-en* from the infinitive.
In the present tense, the PV of the 2nd person singular is:

stem + *t*: *u woont*   you live
       u werkt   you work

The same is true for the PV of the 3rd person singular:

stem + *t*: *John woont in Amsterdam*   John lives in Amsterdam
       Kees studeert in Amsterdam   Kees studies in Amsterdam

The examples below give a survey of the formation of the 1st, 2nd and 3rd person singular of the verbs occurring in the dialogue:

ik   *woon in Amsterdam*
u   *woont in Amsterdam*
John King woont in Amsterdam

ik   *studeer Engels*
u   *studeert Engels*
Kees Bergsma studeert Engels

ik   *werk in Nederland*
u   *werkt in Nederland*
John King werkt in Nederland

ik   *kom eens langs*
u   *komt eens langs*
John King komt eens langs

ik   *zeg : 'ja, graag'*
u   *zegt: 'ja, graag'*
John King zegt: 'ja, graag'

2.2.2 *Zijn*

The verb *zijn* ('to be') is one of the verbs with an irregular present tense. No rules can be given for the formation of the PVs of these verbs. The individual cases should simply be learned by heart.

1st person singular	*ik ben Engelsman* (1.9)	I am English
2nd person singular (formal)	*u bent Nederlander* (1.16)	you are Dutch
3rd person singular	*dat is mijn taal* (1.6)	that is my native language
	mijn naam is John King (1.32)	my name is John King

2.3   SENTENCE STRUCTURES

The order of the various words and word groups in a Dutch sentence is not always fixed. Generally, a certain word order is linked with a certain meaning (sometimes also with a certain intonation), so that a different ordering of the same words usually implies a different meaning.

is uw moeder Nederlandse?	is your mother Dutch?
ja, mijn moeder is Nederlandse	yes, my mother is Dutch

2.3.1 Declarative sentences

Most sentences in the dialogue have the following structure:

Subject +	PV +	remaining constituent	
ik	*woon*	*in Amsterdam* (1.1)	I live in Amsterdam
mijn moeder	*is*	*Engelse* (1.12)	my mother is English
ik	*kom*	*gauw eens langs* (1.33)	I'll drop by soon

These are declarative sentences.

2.3.2 Question sentences

Question sentences can have three possible structures:

1. **PV +**	**subject +**	**remaining constituent**	
studeert	*u*	*Engels?* (1.5)	do you study English?
werkt	*u*	*in Nederland?* (1.20)	do you work in Holland?

Here we are dealing with a yes/no question.

LESSON 2

2. A question sentence can also begin with a question word, such as *wat*, *wie*, *waar*, *wanneer*, *hoe* (meaning respectively 'what', 'who', 'where', 'when', 'how'). This then precedes the PV:

Question word + PV + subject

| *wat* | *zegt* | *u?* (1.26) | what did you say? |
| *waar* | *woont* | *u?* | where do you live? |

3. The same structure can be used as in the declarative sentence, but the intonation (rising at the end of the sentence) and, possibly, a question tag (such as *hè*) make the sentence interrogative. In other question sentences too the intonation can be of this type, but only in this kind of sentence is it obligatory.

subject + PV + remaining constituent + (question tag)

| *u* | *bent Nederlander,* | *hè?* | you are Dutch, aren't you? |
| *u* | *bent Nederlander* | *?* | you are Dutch? |

2.3.3 Imperative sentences

In addition to declarative sentences and question sentences there is also an example of an imperative sentence in the dialogue. Imperative sentences are used to express strong advice, a suggestion, a wish or a command on the part of the speaker. In this lesson we only meet the formal imperative. In this type, the subject (always *u*) **cannot** be left out. The structure is:

PV + subject + remaining constituent

| *komt* | *u* | *eens langs!* (1.25) | why don't you drop by sometime? |

In this example the imperative expresses a loose invitation. The structure is formal because John and Kees do not know each other very well yet.

2.4 *GEEN* E. 9–11

This lesson introduces negation by means of *geen*. *Geen* is a combination of a negation element and an indefinite article. The indefinite article is *een* before count nouns:

een student	a student
een Engelsman	an Englishman
een straat	a street
een adres	an address

Before non-count nouns there is no indefinite article:

Nederlands	Dutch (the language)
Engels	English (the language)
water	water
melk	milk

bent u dan geen Nederlander? (1.8)	aren't you Dutch then?
is uw moeder geen Engelse? (1.13)	is your mother not English?
ik ben geen student	I'm not a student
ik studeer geen Engels	I don't study English

More information about negation can be found in lesson 5, section 2.3.

2.5 ABSENCE OF THE INDEFINITE ARTICLE   E. 1, 2, 5

In Dutch the noun indicating a profession or a nationality after a PV of *zijn* is not preceded by an article, as in the following examples:

ik ben student	I am a student
ik ben journalist	I am a journalist
ik ben Nederlander	I am a Dutchman
mijn moeder is Nederlandse (1.14)	my mother is Dutch
bent u ook student? (1.18)	are you a student as well?

3   FURTHER REMARKS

3.1 *MENEER, MEVROUW, JUFFROUW*

In a formal situation a remark or question is often accompanied by one of the words of address *meneer, mevrouw, juffrouw* to express politeness. These words are followed, if necessary, by the name of the person addressed. (There is more about this in lesson 3.)

uw Nederlands is heel goed, meneer (1.10)	your Dutch is very good, Sir
dank u wel, meneer Bergsma (1.31)	thank you very much, Mr Bergsma

3.2 ADDRESSES, STREETS AND STREETNAMES

In Dutch an address is indicated by first mentioning the name of the street, followed by the house number:

Hoofdweg 8
Leidsestraat 13

LESSON 2

People live *in een straat* (street)   but *op* (or: *aan*) *een plein* (square)
            steeg (alley)   *weg* (road)
            stad (town)   *gracht* (canal)
            land (country)

in de Leidsestraat (1.23)
op de Hoofdweg (1.24)

3.3 NATIONALITIES

Nederland	the Netherlands; Holland
Nederlandse	Dutch woman
Nederlander	Dutchman
Nederlanders (plural)	the Dutch
Nederlands (adjective)	Dutch
Engeland	England
Engelse	English woman
Engelsman	Englishman
Engelsen (plural)	Englishmen
Engels (adjective)	English

LESSON 3

1 SUMMARY OF THE DIALOGUE

Mrs Bergsma meets Mrs Kooiman, an acquaintance of hers, in the Vondelpark. They talk about their children and grandchildren and Mrs Bergsma shows Mrs Kooiman some photographs of her (grand)children.

Pay attention to: – sentences with $\begin{matrix} dit \\ dat \end{matrix}$ + PV*zijn* + remaining constituent

         – *me*
          u   reflexive pronouns
          zich
        – the plural of nouns

2 GRAMMAR

2.1 PRONOUNS
2.1.1 The personal pronouns of the 3rd person singular   E. 2–5

This lesson introduces the 3rd person singular pronoun in subject function. In this function it has three forms: *hij*, *ze* (when stressed *zij*) and *het*. *Hij* refers to one male person, while *ze* (*zij*) refers to one female person:

en wat doet uw zoon? (line 51)	and what does your son do?
hij *is analist* (1.52)	he's an analyst
dat is mijn dochter, **ze** *heet Els* (1.16-17)	that's my daughter. she's called Els

The possessive pronouns corresponding to **hij** and **ze** are **zijn** and **haar** respectively:

hij *heeft* **zijn** *fiets bij zich* (1.37)	he has his bike with him
dit zijn **haar** *kinderen* (1.27)	these are her children

Het occurs in this lesson in a few fixed expressions (see section 3). It is further dealt with in lesson 9.

2.1.2 The reflexive pronouns   E. 9–11, 13

In the sentence *ik heb foto's bij me*, *me* is a reflexive pronoun referring to the same person as the subject, but not having a subject function itself.
The reflexive pronoun corresponding to *ik* is **me**:

ik *heb geen foto's bij* **me** (1.39)	I haven't any photos with me

LESSON 3

The reflexive pronoun corresponding to *u* is also *u:*

*hebt **u** ook foto's bij **u**?* (1.38)	do you have photos with you too?

The reflexive of the 3rd person is *zich*:

*ze heeft nog een kind bij **zich*** (1.24)	she has another child with her
*hij heeft een fiets bij **zich*** (1.37)	he has a bike with him

In this lesson the reflexive pronoun only occurs in the expression *bij zich hebben* ('to have with one').

2.1.3 Survey

The table below gives an overview of the pronoun forms dealt with in this lesson and the previous one.

grammatical person	personal pronoun	possessive pronoun	reflexive pronoun
1	*ik*	*mijn (m'n)*	*me*
2	*u*	*uw*	*u*
3	*hij*	*zijn (z'n)*	*zich*
	ze (zij)	*haar (d'r)*	*zich*
	het	*zijn*	*zich*

N.B. Pay attention to the pronunciation of the possessive pronouns *mijn, zijn, haar* when they are not stressed.

official spelling	semi-official spelling	pronunciation
mijn	*m'n*	/ mən /
zijn	*z'n*	/ zə /
haar	*d'r*	/ ər / or / dər /

2.1.4 The question words *wie* and *wat*   E. 7, 8

Wie and *wat* are question words. *Wie* is used for persons, *wat* for inanimate referents.

*en **wie** is dat?* (1.11)	and who is that?
dat is een vriend van Kees (1.12)	it's a friend of Kees'

***wat** studeert ze?* (1.44)	what does she study?
Nederlands (1.45)	Dutch

Wie and *wat* can be used in the singular as well as in the plural:

wie zijn dat? (1.18)	who are they?
dat zijn mijn kleinkinderen (1.19)	they are my grandchildren
wat zijn dat?	what are they?
dat zijn foto's	they are photos

2.2 VERBS
2.2.1 *Hebben* and *zijn*   E. 12

Like *zijn* (see lesson 2), the verb *hebben* ('to have') has an irregular present tense.
In the singular *hebben* and *zijn* take the following forms:

1st	*ik*	*ben*	I	am	*ik*	*heb*	I	have
2nd	*u*	*bent*	you	are	*u*	*hebt* (also: *u heeft*)	you	have
3rd	*hij*	*is*	he	is	*hij*	*heeft*	he	has
	ze	*is*	she	is	*ze*	*heeft*	she	has
	het	*is*	it	is	*het*	*heeft*	it	has

2.2.2 NEW VERBS

The verbs *doen, gaan, heten* en *kijken* are the new verbs of this lesson. They are regular
verbs; the PVs are formed according to the rules given in lesson 2.

1st	*ik*	*doe*	*ik*	*ga*	*ik*	*kijk*	*ik*	*heet*
2nd	*u*	*doet*	*u*	*gaat*	*u*	*kijkt*	*u*	*heet*
3rd	*hij*	*doet*	*hij*	*gaat*	*hij*	*kijkt*	*hij*	*heet*
	ze	*doet*	*ze*	*gaat*	*ze*	*kijkt*	*ze*	*heet*
	het	*doet*	*het*	*gaat*	*het*	*kijkt*	*het*	*heet*

2.3 NOUNS IN THE PLURAL

The plural of nouns is formed by adding *-en*, *-s* or *-eren* to the singular form. The following rule
serves as a general guideline for the formation of the plural:
- Most nouns of two or more syllables which end in a vowel or in *-el, -em, -en, -er, -je* have *-s*
  in the plural:

foto	– *foto's*	photo(s)
dochter	– *dochters*	daughter(s)
vader	– *vaders*	father(s)
Nederlander	– *Nederlanders*	Dutchman(men)
meisje	– *meisjes*	girl(s)

Nouns ending in a vowel in the singular form their plural by adding an apostrophe *-s*, as with
foto - foto's above, except when they end in *-e* (/ə/), as in *meisje - meisjes*.

– Most other nouns take -*en*:

fiets	– *fietsen*	bike(s)
student	– *studenten*	student(s)
man	– *mannen*	man(men)

If the final consonant of a noun is preceded by a short vowel in the singular, this consonant is doubled in the plural, as is the case with *man* – *mannen* above.
– A very small group of nouns take –*eren*, examples being:

kind	– *kinderen*	child(ren)
ei	– *eieren*	egg(s)

2.4 THE INDEFINITE ARTICLE

The indefinite article *een* occurs before count nouns in the singular, as in:

dat is een vriend van Kees (1.12)	that's a friend of Kees'
Ik heb hier een foto (1.15)	I have a photo here

As in English, there is no indefinite article before
– non-count nouns:

melk	milk
water	water

– plural nouns:

foto's	photos
fietsen	bikes
kinderen	children

2.5 *DIT IS, DAT IS, DIT ZIJN, DAT ZIJN*

Some sentences in Dutch have the following structure:

$$\begin{matrix} dit \\ dat \end{matrix} + \text{PV}zijn + \text{noun phrase}$$

A noun phrase is a phrase containing a noun or proper name.
This type of sentence is used to identify and describe humans or things. The PV (a form of the verb *zijn*) is in the singular or plural, depending on whether the noun phrase is in the singular or plural. *Dit* and *dat* do not change if the PV and the noun phrase are in the plural.

dit is Kees (1.10)	this is Kees
dat is een vriend van Kees (1.12)	that is a friend of Kees'
en wie zijn dat? (1.18)	and who are they?
dat zijn mijn kleinkinderen (1.19)	they're my grandchildren
kijk, dit is mijn boekenkast en dat zijn mijn boeken	look, this is my bookcase and that's my books
kijk, dit is mijn zoon en dat is mijn dochter en dat zijn mijn kleinkinderen	look, this is my son and that's my daughter and that's my grandchildren
wat zijn dat?	what are they?
dat zijn de foto's van mijn huis	they are the photos of my house

3 FURTHER REMARKS

3.1 FORMAL FORMS OF ADDRESS

3.1.1 When you meet someone you know and the situation demands a formal style, you can use the following forms (adding the other person's last name is more formal):

dag meneer
dag meneer Bergsma
dag mevrouw
dag mevrouw Kooiman (1.1)
dag juffrouw
dag juffrouw Van Kampen
goedemorgen meneer
goedemorgen meneer Bergsma
goedemiddag juffrouw
goedemiddag juffrouw Van Kampen
goedeavond mevrouw
goedeavond mevrouw Kooiman

(Normally one does not pronounce the *d* in *goede*; the pronunciation is *goeiemorgen, goeiemiddag, goeieavond.*)

After greeting you may continue with:

hoe gaat het met u? (1.3)

The other person then may say:

goed, dank u, en met u? (1.4-5)

after which you reply:

ook goed

It must be stressed that this is a very formal way of starting a conversation.

LESSON 3

On leaving, you can use the same expressions listed above for greeting, or *tot ziens*.
E.g. in the case of *mevrouw Kooiman:*

dag mevrouw
dag mevrouw Kooiman
goedemiddag mevrouw
goedemiddag mevrouw Kooiman
tot ziens mevrouw
tot ziens mevrouw Kooiman

3.1.2 When you do not know the other person, and the situation demands a formal style, e.g.
when you are in a shop, you may say:

dag meneer
dag mevrouw
dag juffrouw
goedemorgen
goedemiddag
goedeavond

On leaving you may use one of the same expressions.

3.1.3 If you want to ask a stranger something, for instance if you ask somebody the way, you
do not greet the other person, but try to attract their attention by saying:

meneer
pardon meneer
mevrouw
pardon mevrouw
juffrouw
pardon juffrouw

The forms of address in informal settings will be discussed in lesson 4.

3.2 MISCELLANEOUS REMARKS

(1.8) *heel goed*	very well
(1.10) *kijk, dit is Kees*	look, this is Kees
(1.15) *ik heb hier nog een foto*	I have another photo here (= one more photo)
nog een kind (1.24)	one more child
nog een keer (1.35)	again (= one more time)
(see lesson 4, E. 17)	
(1.17) *ze heet Els*	her name is Els; she is called Els
(1.20) *Els heeft drie kinderen*	Els has three children

Here you see the cardinals from 1 to 10. The rest will be treated in lesson 4.

1	– *een*	6	– *zes*
2	– *twee*	7	– *zeven*
3	– *drie*	8	– *acht*
4	– *vier*	9	– *negen*
5	– *vijf*	10	– *tien*

(1.30) *hé, wat leuk!*   hey, that's nice!
       note also: *wat vervelend*   how annoying!
                   wat gek   how odd!
(1.40) *dat is jammer*   that's a pity
(1.53) *hij werkt in een ziekenhuis*   he works in a hospital
(1.54) *o, het is al vier uur!*   oh, it's already four o'clock!
(1.55) *ik ga naar huis*   I'm going home
       naar huis gaan   to go home
       thuis zijn   to be (at) home
(1.58) *de groeten aan uw man*   give my regards to your husband
       (E. 16)

LESSON 4

1 SUMMARY OF THE DIALOGUE

John King calls on Kees Bergsma. Kees gives him a cup of coffee. A friend of Kees' also drops in; her name is Anneke and she studies English. They have coffee together and tell each other where they are from and what they do for a living.

Pay attention to: – the order of the PV and the subject
– imperative sentences
– pronouns
– *de* and *het*

2 GRAMMAR

2.1 PRONOUNS
2.1.1 Personal pronouns – 2nd person singular   E. 3–5, 7, 9

Wilt u een kopje koffie? (line 11)   would you like a cup of coffee?
John, wil je nog een kopje koffie? (1.57)   John, would you like another cup of coffee?

In the first example above you see the 2nd person singular formal pronoun which was discussed in lesson 2. There is also a 2nd person singular informal pronoun, which you can see in the second example. This personal pronoun appears in two forms: *je* and *jij*.
Je is used if the pronoun is unstressed, *jij* is used if it is stressed.

jij bent Engelsman en je spreekt Nederlands (1.45) you are English and you speak Dutch

The corresponding possessive pronouns are *je* (unstressed) and *jouw* (stressed), as in:

doe je jas uit (1.32)   take your coat off
o ja, dit is jouw jas (1.66)   oh yes, this is your coat

2.1.2 Stressed forms   E. 8,9

The stressed forms are always used when two things in the sentence are contrasted:

ik ben Nederlander, jij bent Engelsman (1.44-45) I am Dutch, you are English
hier is jouw jas. nee, dat is mijn jas (1.64-65) here's your coat. no, that's my coat
jouw jas, mijn jas, zijn jas (1.68)   your coat, my coat, his coat

2.1.3 Survey

Here is an overall survey of the singular forms of personal and possessive pronouns. The pronunciation of some unstressed forms is given between obliques.

	personal pronouns		possessive pronouns	
person	without stress	with stress	without stress	with stress
1	*ik*	*ik*	*mijn* /mən/	*mijn*
2 (informal)	*je*	*jij*	*je*	*jouw*
(formal)	*u*	*u*	*uw*	*uw*
3	*hij*	*hij*	*zijn* /zən/	*zijn*
	ze	*zij*	*haar* /ər/, /dər/	*haar*
	het /ət/	*het*	*zijn* /zən/	*zijn*

2.1.4 Using *u* and *je*   E. 1

As regards the use of *u* and *je* the following points should be taken into account:
- the pronoun *u* is used in formal situations but also to express that the speaker respects the person addressed and/or accepts his authority. In the latter case the use of *u* need not always be mutual. Children may, for instance, address their parents as *u*, while their parents call them *je*.
- the use of *je* in addressing parents or older relatives is becoming more widespread, and is also on the increase among younger people in general, even when they meet for the first time.
- normally, a speaker will tend to address a person in the same way as this person addresses him. If you are addressed by *u*, you had better use *u* in your reply.
- the use of *u* corresponds with the use of the surname. If, on the other hand, you address someone by *je*, you will in most cases use his first name.

In general it would be advisable to address every adult person with whom you are not on very intimate terms by *u, meneer, mevrouw* (*juffrouw*). The use of *je* should be limited to friends. This also goes for the use of first names.

2.1.5 Informal forms of address (cf. lesson 3, section 3.1)

When you meet someone and the setting allows an informal style (see section 2.1.4 above), you can say:

dag
hallo
hoi
dag Kees
dag Anneke (1.27)

After greeting you may continue with:

hoe gaat het met je? (1.30)
hoe gaat het?
hoe is het?

LESSON 4

On leaving, you can say:

dag pronunciation /dà-àg/
dag Anneke
dag Kees (1.69)
tot ziens (1.70)
tot ziens Anneke
doeg /doe-oeg/ (becoming increasingly popular)

When two people take leave for only a short time (e.g. for lunch) and they expect to see each other in an hour or so, they usually say *tot straks*.

2.2 VERBS
2.2.1 The PV with *je/jij*   E. 3-5

The PV of the informal 2nd person singular takes the following form:
stem + *t: je woont*
           je werkt

je woont hier fantastisch zeg! (1.24)   hey, you've got a very nice place here!

When *je/jij* comes after the PV, the *t* is not realized. Note the following examples from the dialogue:
daar woon je leuk (1.50)   that's a nice area to live
ben je al lang in Amsterdam? (1.51)   have you been in Amsterdam long?

Note further:
je studeert – *studeer je?*
je komt   – *kom*   *je?*
je doet   – *doe*   *je?*
je gaat   – *ga*   *je?*
je heet   – *heet* *je?*
je vindt   – *vind* *je?*

N.B. In the 2nd and 3rd person singular the PV of verbs with a stem ending in *-d* is *-dt*
      (pronounced /t/):

        vinden: je vindt – *vind je*
                 u   vindt – *vindt u*
                 hij vindt – *vindt hij*
        hoe vind je Nederland? (1.46)   how do you like Holland?

24

2.2.2 *Willen*

The verb *willen* ('to want') has an irregular present tense in that the 3rd person singular does not have a *t*:

ik   wil
je   wilt (also: *je wil*) – *wil je?*
u   wilt
*hij **wil***
*ze   **wil***
*het **wil***

2.3   INVERSION   E. 7, 10–13

In lesson 2 we saw that the structure of the declarative sentence is:

subject + PV   +   remaining constituent
ze   studeert   Engels (1.35)   she studies English

In this lesson a number of sentences with the following structure occur:

**X + PV +subject +remaining
                       constituent**
daar is   de melk   (1.22)   there's the milk
hier heb   ik   de jassen   (1.63)   here are the coats
daar woon je   leuk   (1.50)   that's a nice area to live
dan is   dit   zijn jas   (1.68)   in that case this is his coat
nu   klopt het   (1.69)   now everything's right

The subject now follows the PV. This is because in Dutch the PV is always in second position in the declarative sentence. In other words the PV is always the second constituent of the declarative sentence. If a part of the sentence other than the subject is placed before the PV, the subject will have to move, in order to secure second position for the PV. The subject, then, immediately follows the PV.

ik   ga morgen naar Amsterdam   I'm going to Amsterdam tomorrow
morgen ga ik   naar Amsterdam   tomorrow I'm going to Amsterdam

We call this inversion. It occurs quite frequently in Dutch. However, conjunctions and interjections such as *o, hé, ja, nee, maar, want,* etc. do not cause inversion.
They are placed before the subject:

maar ik heet John (1.15)   but my name is John
nee, ik ben journalist (1.41)   no, I'm a journalist
o, het is al half elf (1.61)   oh, it's already half past ten

N.B. *maar nu moet ik weg* (1.60)   but now I must go
      In this sentense *nu* causes the inversion.

25

LESSON 4

There is more information about inversion in lesson 8, section 2.4.

2.4 THE IMPERATIVE

E. 2

Two types of imperative sentences occur in the dialogue:

1. *komt u binnen* (1.7)   come in, please

This is an example of the formal imperative. It usually expresses an invitation, wish or request, hardly ever a command. The structure is:

PV + subject + remaining constituent
doet   u   uw jas uit (1.9)   take your coat off
gaat   u   zitten! (1.10)   and have a seat

2. *kom binnen* (1.28)   come in

This is the informal imperative addressed to one person. The structure is:

PV 2nd person singular + (infinitive) + remaining constituent(s)
ga   zitten,   Anneke! (1.29)   sit down, Anneke
doe   je jas uit! (1.32)   take your coat off

The use of the formal and informal imperative corresponds with the use of *u* and *je* respectively (see section 2.1.4 above).

2.5 THE GENDER OF NOUNS AND THE DEFINITE ARTICLE

All Dutch nouns have one of two genders:
1. The masculine/feminine gender. In colloqial Dutch there is no difference any more between masculine and feminine. One can take them together as one single gender. All nouns of this gender take *de* as the definite article (singular). We will refer to nouns of this gender as **de-words.**
2. The neuter gender. All nouns of this gender take *het* as definite article (singular). We will refer to nouns of this gender as **het-words.**

Unfortunately, there are no useful rules for predicting whether a noun is a *de*-word or a *het*-word, except:
– nouns indicating male or female humans are *de*-words, except *het meisje* and *het kind*
– all diminutive nouns are *het*-words.

noun	diminutive noun	
de student		student
de journalist		journalist
de vader		father
de dochter	het dochtertje	daughter
de man	het mannetje	man
de jongen	het jongetje	boy
het kind	het kindje	child
–	het meisje	girl
de jas	het jasje	coat, jacket
de kamer	het kamertje	room
het huis	het huisje	house
het boek	het boekje	book

In the plural, *de*-words as well as *het*-words (!) take the definite article *de*.

singular	plural
de dochter	de dochters
het kind	de kinderen
de jas	de jassen
het boek	de boeken

2.6 ADJUNCTS OF TIME AND PLACE   E. 13–16

If both an adjunct of time, e.g. *nu, morgen, vandaag, later* (meaning respectively 'now', 'tomorrow', 'today', 'later'), and an adjunct of place, such as *in Amsterdam, op de Hoofdweg, uit Engeland,* occur in a sentence, the adjunct of time usually precedes the adjunct of place.

	1 time	2 place	
ik kom	morgen	in Amsterdam	I'm coming to Amsterdam tomorrow
ik woon	al lang	in Amsterdam	I've been living in Amsterdam for a long time
ik woon	nu	in de Leidsestraat or:	I live in the Leidsestraat now
nu woon ik		in de Leidsestraat	now I live in the Leidsestraat

An exception to this rule is formed by *daar, hier* and *er,* which precede the adjunct of time, as in:

	1 place	2 time	
woon je	hier	al lang? (1.25)	have you lived here long?
ja, ik woon	hier	al drie jaar (1.26)	yes, I've lived here for three years

LESSON 4

3 FURTHER REMARKS

3.1 *ALSTUBLIEFT* AND *DANK U WEL*

Alstublieft (pronounce:/asty:blieft/) is used:
1. if you hand over something to a person:

alstublieft, meneer King (1.13)	here you are, Mr King

2. when requesting something:

mag ik suiker, alstublieft?	could you pass the sugar, please?

3. if you give an affirmative answer to somebody asking you whether you want to have something:

Anneke, wil je koffie? (1.55)	would you like coffee, Anneke?
alsjeblieft (pronounce: /asjəblieft/) (1.56)	yes, please

Dank u (*wel*) is used:
1. to thank someone (e.g. when he/she opens the door for you)
2. if someone hands you something:

alstublieft, meneer King (1.13)	
dank u wel (1.14)	thank you

3. as a negative reply to someone asking whether you want something:

John, wil je nog een kopje koffie? (1.57)	John, would you like another cup of coffee?
nee, dank je (1.58)	no, thank you

N.B. Whether you say *alstublieft* or *alsjeblieft*, as well as *dank u wel* or *dank je wel*, depends again on whether you address someone with *u* or *je*. Note further that the pronunciation of *alstublieft* is /asty:blieft/ and the pronunciation of *alsjeblieft* is /asjəblieft/.

3.2 MISCELLANEOUS REMARKS

(1.2) *dat is leuk!*	that's nice
(1.7) *komt u binnen*	come in, please
(infinitive: *binnenkomen*)	
(1.9) *doet u uw jas uit*	take your coat off
(infinitive: *uitdoen*)	
(1.10) *gaat u zitten*	please take a seat
(1.37) *zeg maar Anneke, hoor*	just call me Anneke
(1.19) *een beetje melk*	a drop of milk
(1.24) *je woont hier fantastisch, zeg!*	hey, you've got a very nice place here!
(1.25) *woon je hier al lang?*	have you been living here long?
al drie jaar (1.26)	three years

The force of the word *al* here is that three years is considered by Kees to be a long time (cf. 1.26).

(1.29) *je komt precies op tijd voor de koffie*   you're right on time for coffee
(1.33-34) *Anneke, dit is John King*   Anneke, this is John King
      John, dit is Anneke van Kampen   John, this is Anneke van Kampen
      If you introduce a man (or boy) and a woman (or girl) to each other, you begin by
      introducing the man (boy) to the woman (girl).
(1.46) *hoe vind je Nederland?*   how do you like Holland?
(1.52) *bijna een half jaar*   almost six months
(1.54) *ik ben in Amsterdam geboren*   I was born in Amsterdam
(1.60) *nu moet ik weg*   I must go now
(1.61) *het is al half elf*   it's half past ten!
      Here the use of *al* shows that Anneke considers 10.30 to be very late (cf. 1.26).
(1.66) *o ja, dit is jouw jas, pardon*   oh yes, sorry, this is your coat
      Pardon can be used in all formal situations in which an apology is necessary.
      An equivalent is *neemt u mij niet kwalijk*. In informal situations one says *sorry* or
      neem me niet kwalijk. Kees' use of *pardon* in an informal situation (1.66) is now
      definitely out of date. One would expect Kees to say *sorry*.
(1.69) *ja, nu klopt het*   yes, now it's correct
      (*kloppen* in 1.26 = to knock)
(1.72) *tot ziens, welterusten*   good bye, sleep well
      Welterusten is said both by the person going to bed to the other people present and by
      those present to the person who is going to bed.

LESSON 5

1   SUMMARY OF THE DIALOGUE

Mrs Kooiman comes to tea at Mrs de Vries' house. Mrs de Vries' children are helping Mr de Wit in his garden and one of them comes in to get some biscuits. Mrs Kooiman has to leave at 4.30 but she just misses a bus and so has to wait for another one.

Pay attention to: – sentences with *niet* (negation)
                                    – plural personal pronouns and PVs (*we, jullie, ze* + PV)

2   GRAMMAR

2.1   PRONOUNS
2.1.1 The plural personal pronouns   E. 3, 7

In this lesson we treat the plural personal pronouns (but only those forms which are used when the pronoun is the subject of a sentence). The forms are:

person	without stress	with stress
1	we	wij
2 (informal)	jullie	jullie
(formal)	u	u
3	ze	zij

we hebben honger mam (line 34)	we're hungry, mum
willen jullie een koekje? (1.35)	would you (plural) like a biscuit?
ze spelen bij de buren (1.13)	they're playing at the neighbours'
wij hebben geen tuin, maar zij hebben wel een tuin (1.23)	we haven't got a garden, but they do have a garden

2.2   VERBS
2.2.1 The plural of the PV   E. 2–4

In the examples of 2.1 the plural of the PV in the present tense consists, for all three persons, of stem + (*e*)*n*. These forms are identical with the infinitive. This does not apply to *u*. The PV of *u* is stem + *t* in the singular as well as in the plural. The present tense of a regular verb, then, is as follows (the subject forms of the pronouns are added):

person		stem + -en		stem +-n	
singular:	1	ik	werk	ik	zie
	2 (informal)	je	werkt/werk je?	je	ziet/zie je?
	(formal)	u	werkt	u	ziet
	3	hij	werkt	hij	ziet
		ze	werkt	ze	ziet
		het	werkt	het	ziet
plural:	1	we	werken	we	zien
	2 (informal)	jullie	werken	jullie	zien
	(formal)	u	werkt	u	ziet
	3	ze	werken	ze	zien

With irregular verbs like *hebben, willen* and *zijn* the plural of the PV in the present tense is also identical with the infinitive.

person		hebben		zijn		willen	
singular	1	ik	heb	ik	ben	ik	wil
	2 (informal)	je	hebt/heb je?	je	bent/ben je?	je	wilt/wil je?
	(formal)	u	hebt	u	bent	u	wilt
	3	hij	heeft	hij	is	hij	wil
		ze	heeft	ze	is	ze	wil
		het	heeft	het	is	het	wil
plural:	1	we	hebben	we	zijn	we	willen
	2 (informal)	jullie	hebben	jullie	zijn	jullie	willen
	(formal)	u	hebt	u	bent	u	wilt
	3	ze	hebben	ze	zijn	ze	willen

2.3 NEGATION
E. 9–13

2.3.1 In lesson 2 we encountered negation by means of *geen. Geen* is a combination of a negation element and an indefinite article. In all other cases we use *niet* to make a (part of a) sentence negative.

ik heb een boek	I have a book
ik heb geen boek	I have no book
ik heb het boek	I have the book
ik heb het boek niet	I don't have the book
ik heb boeken	I have books
ik heb geen boeken	I have no books
ik heb de boeken	I have the books
ik heb de boeken niet	I don't have the books

2.3.2 The place of *niet* in the sentence
The negation may apply to:
1. the whole sentence (sentence negation)
2. a constituent of the sentence (constituent negation)

31

LESSON 5

The place of *niet* in the sentence is determined according to whether it has a sentence negation function or a constituent negation function.

2.3.3 Sentence negation

In the case of sentence negation *niet* comes after:
1. the PV

dank u, ik rook niet (1.30)	thank you, I don't smoke

2. object

ik zie Corrie niet (1.18)	I don't see Corrie

3. adjunct of time without preposition

ik zie Corrie morgen niet	I won't see Corrie tomorrow

4. *er, hier, daar*

de jongen is er niet	the boy isn't there

5. the NP of the identity construction (cf. lesson 3, section 2.5)

maar dat is lijn 15 niet (1.62)	but that isn't the 15

But it comes before:
1. a preposition

nee, we studeren niet in Amsterdam	no, we don't study in Amsterdam

2. *binnen, buiten, beneden, boven, thuis* (respectively 'inside', 'outside', 'downstairs', 'upstairs', 'at home')

zijn de kinderen niet thuis? (1.12)	aren't the children at home?

3. an adjective (possibly preceded by an adverb), if the adjective follows subject and PV

nee, het balkon is niet groot	no, the balcony isn't big
ja, maar het balkon is niet erg groot (1.27)	yes, but the balcony isn't very big

2.3.4 Constituent negation
In this case *niet* is placed before the constituent which is to be made negative. Often this constituent is stressed:

ik kom niet vandáág maar mórgen	I'm not coming today but tomorrow

N.B. *Niet* never comes before the PV, not even when the PV bears stress:

ik lóóp niet, ik fiéts	I don't walk, I cycle

See Appendix C2 for more information on negation.

3 FURTHER REMARKS

3.1 TELLING THE TIME (*KLOKKIJKEN*)   E.15,17

For the purpose of telling the time, the Dutch divide the face of the clock in two:

When the minute-hand of the clock is in the upper half, the point of reference is the whole hour. When the minute-hand is in the lower half, the point of reference is the half hour (the same point where the hour-hand is at six o'clock). Sometimes, but less frequently, the reference is the whole hour here too.

10.00	*het is tien uur*	it's ten o'clock
9.50	*het is tien (minuten) voor tien*	it's ten to ten
10.10	*het is tien (minuten) over tien*	it's ten past ten
9.45	*het is kwart voor tien*	it's a quarter to ten
10.15	*het is kwart over tien*	it's a quarter past ten
10.30	*het is half elf*	it's half past ten
10.20	*het is tien (minuten) voor half elf/*	it's twenty past ten
	het is twintig over tien	
10.25	*het is vijf (minuten) voor half elf*	it's twenty-five past ten
10.35	*het is vijf (minuten) over half elf*	it's twenty-five to eleven
10.40	*het is tien (minuten) over half elf/*	it's twenty to eleven
	het is twintig voor elf	

In official time indication (e.g. at railway stations and airports), the 24 hour system is used.

11.27 in the morning: 11.27 (read as *elf uur zevenentwintig*)
11.27 at night   : 23.27 (read as *drieëntwintig uur zevenentwintig*)

N.B.	*hoe laat is het?*	what's the time?
	het is half vijf	it's half past four
	hoe laat komt je man thuis?	when does your husband come home?
	om half zes komt mijn man	
	thuis (1.56)	my husband comes home at half past five

LESSON 5

3.2 PREPOSITIONS

Note the following prepositions occurring in the dialogue:

(ze spelen) **bij** *de buren* (1.12)	(they're playing) at the neighbours'
in *de tuin* (1.13)	in the garden
op *het gras* (1.17)	on the lawn
onder *de boom* (1.20)	under the tree
(ik ga weer) **naar** *de tuin* (1.49)	(I'm going back) to the garden

3.3 *THUIS* AND *NAAR HUIS*

zijn de kinderen niet **thuis?** (1.12)	aren't the children at home?
ik ga **naar huis**	I'm going home
om half zes komt mijn man **thuis** (1.57)	my husband comes home at half past five

3.4 *TOCH*

u hebt toch een balkon? (1.26)	but you do have a balcony, don't you?

One of the many meanings of unstressed *toch* is that it expresses a presumption on the part of the speaker that is in contrast with what somebody else has said or implied:

waar werk je?	where do you work?
ik wérk toch niet. ik ben student	but I don't work. I'm a student
heb je een sigaret?	have you got a cigarette?
maar je róókt toch niet?	but you don't smoke, do you?
kom je altijd met de auto?	do you always come by car?
maar ik héb toch geen auto!	but I haven't got a car!

3.5 MISCELLANEOUS REMARKS

(1.22) **heel** *vaak* — very often

(1.27) *ja, maar het balkon is niet erg groot* — yes, but the balcony is not very big

    Heel and *erg* are adverbs occurring in combination with an adjective or adverb in order to emphasize it.

(1.23–24) *wij hebben geen tuin* — we haven't got a garden

      en de buren wel — and the neighbours have

    Wel is used here as an affirmative particle contrasting with *niet/geen.*

(1.28) *daarom spelen ze liever in de tuin*

    The adverb *liever* is the comparative of the adverb *graag:*

    ze spelen **graag** *op het balkon,* — they **like** playing on the balcony,

    maar ze spelen **liever** *in de tuin* — but they **prefer** playing in the garden

(1.33) *wat is er?* — what's the matter?

(1.34) *we* **hebben** *honger, mam* — we're hungry, mum

The Dutch say: *ik heb honger*   I am hungry

                 ik heb dorst   I am thirsty

(1.44) *mag ik **nog een** koekje?*   may I have another biscuit?

(1.61) *daar komt **weer een** bus*   there comes another bus

Nog een means 'one in addition to the quantity which is already there'.

Weer een means 'one more in a series of objects or events' (refers to time).

ik ga weer naar de tuin (1.41)   I'm going back to the garden

(1.57) *ach, de bus gaat net weg*   ah, the bus is just pulling out

(1.68) *bedankt voor uw bezoek*   thanks for your visit

Bedankt is less formal than *dank u wel*.

LESSON 6

1 SUMMARY OF THE DIALOGUE

John King is having a cup of coffee on the terrace of a café. A passer-by asks a policeman who is also sitting there where the Emmastraat is. The policeman explains how to get there by public transport. Then John strikes up a conversation with the policeman, who tells him about his work. John asks the policeman which tram he should take to get to the Hoofdweg.

2 GRAMMAR

2.1 *WELK/WELKE*   E. 1–14, 11

Welk(e) is a question word. It means 'which' as well as 'what'. It takes two forms:
1. *welk* , used in combination with – *het*-words
2. *welke,* used in combination with – *de*-words
                                   – all plural nouns

het nummer	*welk nummer*
de nummers	*welke nummers*
de tram	*welke tram*
de trams	*welke trams*
het meisje	*welk meisje*
de meisjes	*welke meisjes*

bij welk postkantoor? (line 13)	at which post office?
welk nummer op de Hoofdweg? (1.59)	what number on the Hoofdweg?
en bij welke halte is de Emmastraat? (1.34)	and what stop do I need for the Emmastraat?

Welk(e) is usually followed by a noun. However, it is also possible to use it independently; in such cases it refers to a noun which has been mentioned before but is not repeated in the sentence in question.

ik neem de tram	I take the tram
welke? (= welke tram neem je?)	which one? (= which tram do you take?)
geef je boek eens	give me your book, will you?
welk? (= welk boek wil je hebben?)	which one? (= which book do you want?)
de foto's zijn heel mooi	the photos are very nice
welke? (= welke foto's zijn heel mooi?)	which ones? (= which photos are very nice?)

N.B. The pronunciation of *welk* is usually /welək/.

2.2 *DIENST* AND *VRIJ*
2.2.1 *Dienst*

In this lesson the word *dienst* occurs several times, and with different meanings:

1. *tot uw dienst* (1.38)   you're welcome

This is used as a reply when somebody thanks you for a service you have done him/her. It is not used if somebody thanks you when you have given him something (cf. 1.8–9 of the dialogue). Instead of *tot uw dienst* you can also say *geen dank* or *graag gedaan*.

2. *maar vanmiddag heb ik dienst* (1.46)   but this afternoon I am on duty

Dienst here means 'working hours'.
Ik heb dienst is used in most cases by people who have a function in which they wear a uniform.

mijn diensten zijn onregelmatig (1.48)	I have irregular working hours
nachtdienst	night duty
weekenddienst	weekend duty
ploegendienst	shift system

The structure of the sentence *ik heb dienst* is

subject + PV (*hebben*) + noun phrase

It is the same structure as in:

ik heb honger (see lesson 5, section 3.3)
ik heb dorst
ik heb vrij

The negative is formed by means of *geen*:

ik heb geen honger
ik heb geen dorst
ik heb geen vrij
ik heb geen dienst

2.2.2 *Vrij*   E. 7, 8

In this lesson the word *vrij*, too, has several meanings:

1. *is deze plaats vrij?* (1.1)   is this seat taken?

2. *nee, ik heb vanmorgen vrij* (1.45)   no, I'm off duty this morning

*ik **heb** vrij*   I do not have to work
                                              negative: *ik heb **geen** vrij*

LESSON 6

*ik **ben** vrij*

1. I do not have to work (so the same as above)

2. I am independent, free
negative: *ik ben **niet** vrij*

2.3 VANMIDDAG, 'S MIDDAGS, MIDDAG ETC.   E. 7–9
2.3.1 The Dutch divide the day into 4 periods:
from   6 to 12 hours is *de morgen* or *ochtend* (the morning)
from 12 to 18 hours is *de middag*   (the afternoon)
from 18 to 24 hours is *de avond*   (the evening)
from 24 to   6 hours is *de nacht*   (the night)

2.3.2 *vanmorgen/vanochtend*   this morning
    vanmiddag   this afternoon
    vanavond   this evening
    vannacht   tonight
    vandaag   today
    gisteren   yesterday
    eergisteren   the day before yesterday
    morgen   tomorrow
    overmorgen   the day after tomorrow

N.B. *morgen* -1. tomorrow
           2. morning
    *morgen**ochtend*** – tomorrow morning

2.3.3 *'s morgens/'s ochtends*   in the morning
    's middags   in the afternoon
    's avonds   in the evening
    's nachts   at night
    overdag   in the daytime; by day
soms werk ik 's morgens (1.49)   sometimes I work in the morning
soms werk ik 's middags (1.50)   sometimes I work in the afternoon
soms werk ik 's avonds (1.51)   sometimes I work in the evening
soms werk ik 's nachts (1.52)   sometimes I work at night
's nachts slaapt hij, maar overdag werkt hij   at night he sleeps, but in the daytime he works

3   FURTHER REMARKS

3.1   WEL
Wel has many meanings in Dutch. Two of them occur in the dialogue in this lesson:

1. Stressed *wel* may express or reinforce the positive force of a statement. It is often used, explicity or implicitly, in contrast with another statement:

38

vindt u dat prettig? (1.53)	do you like that?
ik wél, maar mijn vrouw niét (1.54–55)	I do, but not my wife
u kunt wél met de tram	you can go to the Emmastraat by tram
maar niét met de bus naar de Emmastraat	but not by bus
ik heb géén honger maar wél dorst	I'm not hungry but I am thirsty
wij hebben géén tuin maar de buren wél	we haven't got a garden but the neighbours do have one
is deze plaats vrij? (1.1)	is this seat taken?
ja, ik geloof het wél (1.2)	yes, I think it is

2. Unstressed *wel* may express a willingness on the part of the speaker to do something:

dan ga ik wel met de bús (1.24)	then I'll take the bus
ik hélp u wel even	I'll give you a hand
ik bréng je wel even thuis	I'll take you home
nee, ik neem wel een táxi	no, I'll take a taxi
ik betaal je koffie wel	I'll pay for your coffee

3.2   MISCELLANEOUS REMARKS

(1.4) *ik kom bij u, meneer*   *I'll be with you, Sir*
(1.5) *één koffie, alstublieft*
     This utterance does not have the structure of a complete sentence. Its meaning, however, is that of a full sentence. It means: *mag ik een kopje koffie van u?* ('could I have a cup of coffee, please?')

(1.9) *hoeveel krijgt u?*	how much do I owe you?
(1.10) *tachtig cent, alstublieft (f 0,80)*	eighty cents, please

1 cent	–	(*f 0,01*)
5 cent	– *een stuiver*	(*f 0,05*)
10 cent	– *een dubbeltje*	(*f 0,10*)
25 cent	– *een kwartje*	(*f 0,25*)
100 cent	– *een gulden*	(*f 1,00*)
250 cent	– *een rijksdaalder*	(*f 2,50*)
10 gulden	– *een tientje*	(*f 10,00*)

(1.16) *weet u de Emmastraat?*	do you know how to get to the Emmastraat?
see also lesson 8, section 2.2.1	
(1.17) *eens kijken*	let me think
(1.20) *bent u met de auto?*	are you by car?
dan ga ik wel met de bus (1.24)	in that case I think I'll go by bus
nee, alleen met de tram (1.26)	no, only by tram

Here are some more examples:

met de trein	by train
met de taxi	by taxi
met het vliegtuig	by air
met de boot	by boat
met/op de fiets	by bike/on the bike
met/op de brommer	on the moped
(E. 9)	

(1.29) *lijn 16 stopt bij de Dam*   tram 16 stops near the Dam

(1.33) *achter het paleis*   behind the palace

(1.39) *u bent **zeker** Amsterdammer?*   you're an Amsterdammer, **I presume?**

(1.40) *u weet zo goed de weg*   you know your way about so well

(1.42) *ik kom uit Rotterdam*

This sentence has two possible readings. First it can mean 'I have just arrived from Rotterdam'; secondly it can be understood as 'I come from Rotterdam', (i.e. it's my hometown/my birthplace). In this context 1.42 means 'I come from Rotterdam'.

(1.43) *ik ben hier **bij** de politie*   I am with the police here

(1.62) *o, dat is **dichtbij** de brug*   oh, that's **near** the bridge

dichtbij, vlakbij   near, close by

In this case, *dichtbij* is a preposition (E. 12). It may also be used as an adverb. The opposite of *dichtbij* is *ver weg*, which can only be used as an adverb:

adverb:

is de halte dichtbij?	is the stop nearby?
nee, de halte is ver weg	no, the stop is a long way away

preposition:

het postkantoor is dichtbij/vlakbij het ziekenhuis	the post office is near the hospital

LESSON 7

1 SUMMARY OF THE DIALOGUE

Els and Jaap go to Rotterdam for the day by train. Jaap has to attend a meeting and Els goes to a museum. Their children are with the neighbours. At the station they see Kees. He's waiting for two boys who are due to arrive from Antwerp.

Pay attention to the plural possessive pronouns: *ons/onze*

jullie/je
(uw)
hun

2 GRAMMAR

2.1 PRONOUNS   E. 3–5, 8–13
2.1.1 The plural possessive pronouns

The possessive pronoun of the 1st person plural is *ons* or *onze*.

ons   is used before: – *het*-words in the singular
onze is used before: – *de*-words
– all plural nouns

(cf. *welk/welke*)

ik zie het boek	*welk boek?*	*ons boek*
ik zie de trein	*welke trein?*	*onze trein*
ik zie de boeken	*welke boeken?*	*onze boeken*
ik zie de treinen	*welke treinen?*	*onze treinen*

is dat onze trein? (line 26)   is that our train?
de kinderen spelen graag met ons   the children like playing with the girl next door
               buurmeisje (1.65)

The possessive pronoun of the 2nd person plural is *jullie* or *je*:
waar zijn jullie kinderen? (1.60)   where are your children?

Je is used when the possessive pronoun immediately follows the personal pronoun *jullie:*
zien jullie je handschoenen niet?   can't you see your gloves?

The possessive pronoun of the 3rd person plural is *hun:*
is dat het huis van Els en Jaap?   is that Els and Jaap's house?
ja, dat is hun huis   yes, that's their house

LESSON 7

2.1.2 Survey

The table below gives all the subject forms of personal pronouns with the corresponding possessive pronoun forms.

			personal pronouns (subject form)	possessive pronouns
singular:	1		ik	mijn /mən/
	2	(informal)	jij, je	jouw, je
		(formal)	u	uw
	3		hij	zijn /zən/
			zij, ze	haar /ər/, /dər/
			het /ət/	zijn /zən/
plural:	1		wij, we	ons, onze
	2	(informal)	jullie	jullie, je
		(formal)	u	uw
	3		zij, ze	hun

2.1.3 The personal pronoun 3rd person singular masculine *hij* is pronounced   E. 3–5, 13
/ie/ when it bears no stress and at the same time is not the first constituent of
the sentence. However, it is invariably spelt *hij*.
heeft – /ie/?
hoe laat vertrekt – /ie/?
staat – /ie/ *daar?*

2.2. VERBS
2.2.1 Verbs with a fixed preposition

There are a number of verbs which are accompanied by a fixed preposition. Two of them are to be found in the dialogue, *praten met* and *wachten op:*

kijk, nu praat hij met de conducteur (1.37)   look, now he's talking to the guard
ik wacht op twee jongens uit België (1.41)   I'm waiting for two boys from Belgium

The object immediately follows the preposition. We call the combination of preposition +
object a prepositional object.

2.2.2 Pay attention to the spelling of the following verbs:

	vinden		*wachten*		*praten*		*zitten*
singular: 1 ik	vind	ik	wacht	ik	praat	ik	zit
2 je	vindt, vind je	je	wacht, wacht je	je	praat, praat je	je	zit, zit je
u	vindt	u	wacht	u	praat	u	zit
3 hij	vindt	hij	wacht	hij	praat	hij	zit
ze	vindt	ze	wacht	ze	praat	ze	zit
het	vindt	het	wacht	het	praat	het	zit

plural:
1	*we*	*vinden*	*we*	*wachten*	*we*	*praten*	*we*	*zitten*
2	*jullie*	*vinden*	*jullie*	*wachten*	*jullie*	*praten*	*jullie*	*zitten*
	u	*vindt*	*u*	*wacht*	*u*	*praat*	*u*	*zit*
3	*ze*	*vinden*	*ze*	*wachten*	*ze*	*praten*	*ze*	*zitten*

See also lesson 4, section 2.2.1
            lesson 2, section 2.2.3

2.3 *NU* AND *NOU*

a) *nu* – at this moment, now
b) *nou* is used:
1. to express impatience

kom nou! (1.6)   come along!/hurry up!

2. to express amazement

wat zoeken jullie daar nou toch? (1.48)   what are you going there for?

3. to draw attention and signal that one is going to say something; it can also be used simply to give the speaker time to think:

nou ... dat zit zo   well ... it's like this

In colloquial speech people often use *nou* to mean 'at this moment'. The use of *nu* in contexts as described under b) is thought to be affected usage.

2.4 *PRATEN* AND *SPREKEN*

Praten and *spreken* can often be used synonymously. However, even when they have the same meaning, *spreken* is generally regarded as slightly more formal.

hij praat met de conducteur   he is talking to the guard
hij spreekt met de conducteur
hij praat over de Picasso-tentoonstelling   he is talking about the Picasso exhibition
hij spreekt over de Picasso-tentoonstelling

Sometimes *spreken* can have different meanings. Note the following examples:

een politicus spreekt dikwijls voor een   a politician often talks before a large
                 groot publiek   audience
hij praat veel   he talks a lot
hij praat Engels   he's speaking English (i.e. at the moment)
hij spreekt goed Engels   he speaks good English
                                      (i.e. he can speak good English)

spreekt u Nederlands?   do you speak Dutch?
(in een telefoongesprek:) met wie spreek ik?   (in a telephone conversation:) who's speaking,
                    met Kees Bergsma   please? Kees Bergsma

kan ik mevrouw Kooiman even spreken?   could I speak to Mrs Kooiman, please?

Iemand spreken is often synonymous with *iemand ontmoeten, iemand zien,* as in:

ik spreek/zie hem vanavond nog wel   I'll see him tonight at the meeting
        op de vergadering

3 FURTHER REMARKS

(1.4) *ik kom zo*   I'll be with you in a minute

(1.6) *het is **zeker** een half uur naar het*   it is at least half an hour to the
        station   station

(1.8) ***over** 40 minuten gaat de trein*   the train leaves in 40 minutes

(1.11) ***net** op tijd*   just in time (i.e. you almost missed it)

(1.13) ***precies** op tijd*   right on time (i.e. you came at the right
        moment)

(1.23) *om half negen **precies***   at eight-thirty precisely

(1.12) *ze komen met de trein*   they are coming by train

(1.29) *wij gaan met de sneltrein*   we are taking a fast train
    NS (Nederlandse Spoorwegen), the Dutch state railways, use the term *'intercity'*
instead of *sneltrein.*

(1.30) *zeg, daar staat Kees*   hey, there's Kees

(1.31) *wel nee, dat is Kees niet*   oh no, that isn't Kees

(1.33) *de man met de hoed bedoel ik niet*   I don't mean the man with the hat
    (E. 7)

(1.49) *Jaap moet naar een vergadering*   Jaap has to go to a meeting

(1.66) *zeg, jullie trein vertrekt*   hey, your train's leaving

(1.67) *goede reis*   have a good journey

LESSON 8

1 SUMMARY OF THE DIALOGUE

John King goes to the library to look for a certain book on the history of Amsterdam. The librarian helps him. There are very many books on Amsterdam in the library. She also gives John information concerning the lending out of books, the reading room and the opening hours of the library.

Pay attention to the demonstratives *deze, die, dit, dat.*

2 GRAMMAR

2.1 DEMONSTRATIVE PRONOUNS
2.1.1 Forms

The demonstrative pronouns are: *dit*   (this)
                                  dat   (that)
                                  deze (this, these)
                                  die   (that, those)

Dit and *dat* are used before, or instead of: singular *het*-words
Deze and *die* are used before, or instead of: singular *de*-words
                                          all plural nouns

2.1.2 Meaning   E. 4–7, 9
2.1.2.1 Distance

Like English 'this' and 'these', *dit* and *deze* are connected with the notion *hier, dichtbij*, i.e. the person or object in question is relatively close to the speaker.
Like English 'that' and 'those', *die* and *dat* are connected with *daar, verder weg*, i.e. the person or object in question is further away from the speaker.

	hier	**daar**
het boek	*dit boek*	*dat boek*
de tafel	*deze tafel*	*die tafel*
de boeken	*deze boeken*	*die boeken*
de tafels	*deze tafels*	*die tafels*

die juffrouw helpt u wel (line 16)   that lady will help you
dit nummer, juffrouw (1.19)   this number, Miss
het boek staat in die kast (1.13)   the book is in that bookcase
deze zaal is net nieuw (1.50)   this is a new room
deze boeken ken ik (1.25)   I know these books

LESSON 8

2.1.2.2 Something already mentioned

E. 3, 13

If one refers to something already mentioned, one uses *die* and *dat:*

hebt u dat boek? (1.9)	have you got that book? (i.e.the book already mentioned, *'Amsterdam vroeger en nu'*)
ja, dat boek hebben we (1.11)	yes, we've got that book
ik zoek de Telegraaf *hebt u die krant?*	I'm looking for the *Telegraaf* have you got it? (= that newspaper)
kent u meneer Bergsma? *ja, die man ken ik wel*	do you know Mr Bergsma? yes, I know him (that man)

2.1.2.3 Differentiation

When you are talking about, for instance, two objects of the same type, and you want to differentiate between them, you can use *deze* and *die* (or, in the case of a *het*-word, *dit* and *dat*) alternately. In such a case *deze/die* and *dit/dat* do not express a difference in distance from the speaker.

ik heb hier twee kranten *welke wilt U? deze krant* *of die krant?*	I have two newspapers here which one do you want? this one or this one?
welke foto's zijn van u? *deze foto's of die foto's?*	which photos are yours? these ones or these ones?
dit boek is wel interessant *maar dat boek niet*	this book is interesting but this one isn't

2.1.3 Independent use of the demonstratives

Dit, dat, deze and *die* may also be used independently. The noun in question may be left out if it is clear from the context what is meant.

welk boek? o, dat (boek) (1.27–28)	which book? oh, that one
welke? deze (1.56–57)	which books? these ones
die kunnen we niet uitlenen (1.59)	we can't lend those ones out

2.1.4 *Dat* and *die* as personal pronoun substitutes

E. 11, 12

Dat and *die* (but not *deze* and *dit!*) may also be used to replace a personal pronoun (in subject as well as in object function) of the 3rd person. In such cases the meaning aspect of *'daar'*, *'ver weg'* is not present. *Dat* replaces *het*, and *die* replaces the other personal pronouns of the 3rd person. They are not followed by a noun. (There is more about this in lessons 14 and 15, and in appendix D2.)

subject function

waar is Jaap?	where is Jaap?
die *is naar een vergadering*	he's gone to a meeting
(*die* replaces *hij*)	
waar is Els?	where is Els?
die *zit in de tuin*	she's sitting in the garden
(*die* replaces *ze* singular)	
hebben Jaap en Els een auto?	have Jaap and Els got a car?
nee, **die** *hebben geen auto*	no, they haven't got a car
(*die* replaces *ze* plural)	

object function

leest u dit boek?	are you reading this book?
nee, **dat** *lees ik niet*	no, I'm not reading it
(*dat* replaces *het*)	
kent u deze man?	do you know this man?
nee, **die** *ken ik niet*	no, I don't know him
(*die* replaces *hem*)	
zoekt u deze boeken?	are you looking for these books?
nee, **die** *zoek ik niet*	no, I'm not looking for them
(*die* replaces *ze*)	

N.B. *Die* and *dat* always precede the PV, and consequently take front position in the sentence.

Dat in 1.24 refers to the whole previous sentence. It should be translated by 'that'.

2.2 VERBS
2.2.1 *Kennen, weten, kunnen*

Pay attention to the meanings of these three verbs.
Kennen means 'to be acquainted with', 'to be aware of'.
Weten means 'to have specific knowledge concerning a certain person or subject'.

deze boeken **ken** *ik* (1.24)	I know these books
ken *je die film?*	do you know that film?
ken *je John King?*	do you know John King?
ja, ik **ken** *hem wel,*	yes, I know him,
maar ik **weet** *niet waar hij woont*	but I don't know where he lives
en **ken** *je die dame daar?*	and do you know that woman there?
nee, die **ken** *ik niet*	no, I don't know her
ik **weet** *niet wie dat is*	I don't know who she is
weet *je de Emmastraat?*	do you know how to get to the Emmastraat?
ken *je de Emmastraat?*	do you know the Emmastraat?

LESSON 8

*ik **weet** wel wat de titel is,*	I know what the title is,
*maar ik **weet** niet wie de schrijver is*	but I don't know who the author is
waar is Kees?	where is Kees?
*dat **weet** ik niet*	I don't know
de restaurants zijn vandaag niet open	the restaurants aren't open today
*hoe **weet** je dat?*	how do you know?
dat staat in de krant	it's in the newspaper
wanneer komt John langs?	when's John coming to see you?
*misschien vanavond wel. wie **weet!***	maybe tonight. who knows?

Kunnen means 'to be able', 'to be possible':

*juffrouw, **kan** ik dit boek lenen?* (1.52)	can I borrow this book, Miss?
*ja, dat **kan*** (1.54)	yes, you can
***ken** je Nederlands?*	do you know Dutch?
*ik **kan** het lezen,*	I can read it,
*maar ik **kan** het nog niet spreken*	but I can't speak it yet
ik wil met de bus naar de Emmastraat	I want to take a bus to the Emmastraat
***kan** dat?*	is that possible?
*nee, dat **kan** niet*	no, it's not possible
*u **kunt** alleen met de tram*	you can only get there by tram
or: *dat **kan** alleen met de tram*	it's only possible by tram

2.2.2 Forms of *kunnen* E. 1, 2, 13, 14

The present tense of the verb *kunnen* is irregular in the singular but regular in the plural.

ik   *kan*
jij   *kunt, kun je,* (*je kan, kan je* also occurs)
u   *kunt* (*u kan* also occurs)
hij   *kan*
ze   *kan*
het   *kan*
we   *kunnen*
jullie kunnen
u   *kunt* (*u kan* also occurs)
ze   *kunnen*

2.3 AUXILIARY + MAIN VERB E. 1, 2, 13, 14

If the verb phrase of a sentence consists of an auxiliary verb plus the infinitive of the main verb, the infinitive goes to the end of the sentence.

48

*kunt u mijn boeken niet **vinden?*** (1.38)	can't you find my books?
*hier **kunt** u rustig **lezen*** (1.51)	here you can read quietly
*u **kunt** hier tot 5 uur **blijven*** (1.62)	you can stay here until 5 o'clock

2.4 INVERSION

Often a declarative sentence does not begin with the subject, but with an adverbial phrase (indicating time, place etc.) or even with the object. However, one cannot have two adverbial phrases at the beginning of a sentence since the PV always goes second (cf. lesson 4, section 2.3).

There may be many reasons for putting another constituent than the subject at the beginning of a sentence. Here are a few:

1. Making a direct link with the topic that has already been mentioned in the previous sentence

*ik woon **in de Leidsestraat***	I live in the Leidsestraat
***daar** woon je leuk*	that's a nice area to live
*u kunt hier tot **vijf uur** blijven*	you can stay here until 5 o'clock
***dan** gaat de bibliotheek dicht*	that's when the library closes
we gaan vanmiddag naar het museum	we're going to the museum this afternoon
***dan** eten we in een restaurant*	then we're going to eat in a restaurant
*en **daarna** gaan we weer naar huis*	and after that we're going back home
*'**Amsterdam vroeger en nu***'.	'Amsterdam vroeger en nu'.
hebt u dat boek?	do you have that book?
*ja, **dat boek** hebben we, meneer*	yes, we have it, Sir
*kent u **meneer Bergsma?***	do you know Mr Bergsma?
*nee, **die** ken ik niet*	no, I don't know him
*weet u **het nummer** van het boek?*	do you know the number of the book?
*nee, **dat** heb ik niet*	no, I don't have it
*wat vind je van **deze tekeningen?***	what do you think of these drawings?
***die** vind ik heel erg mooi*	I find them very nice
*is **deze plaats vrij?***	is this seat taken?
***dat** geloof ik wel*	I think so
*is de **bibliotheek zondags ook open?***	is the library open on Sundays too?
***dat** weet ik niet*	I don't know

2. Presenting a point of departure for the sentence; the speaker uses the rest of the sentence progressively to narrow down what he is trying to say. (When used in this way, the first constituent can be called a frame, and the remainder of that sentence an insert for that frame.)

in deze kast staan veel boeken over Amsterdam
in this case there are a lot of books about Amsterdam

op dinsdagavond is de bibliotheek van zeven tot tien open
on Tuesday evenings the library is open from seven till ten

in de leeszaal kunt u rustig lezen
in the reading room you can read quietly

in Antwerpen spreken ze geen Frans maar Nederlands
in Antwerp they don't speak French but Dutch

dichtbij het postkantoor is een halte van lijn 1
near the post office is a tramstop for line 1

vanavond moet ik naar een vergadering
tonight I have to go to a meeting

in de tuin van de buren staan geen bomen
in the neighbours' garden there are no trees

op 20 april ga ik met de boot naar Engeland
on 20 April I'm going by boat to England

boeken over geschiedenis vind ik altijd heel interessant
books about history I always find very interesting

een fiets kan je in Nederland niet voor 100 gulden krijgen
you can't get a bike in Holland for 100 guilders

woordenboeken kunnen we niet uitlenen
we can't lend dictionaries out

3. Extra emphasis, mostly for contrast

soms werk ik 's morgens,
soms werk ik 's middags
en soms werk ik 's avonds

sometimes I work in the morning,
sometimes I work in the afternoon
and sometimes I work in the evening

hier is de suiker en daar is de melk
here's the sugar and there's the milk

in Utrecht heb je geen trams,
maar in Den Haag wel

in Utrecht there are no trams,
but there are in The Hague

vanmorgen heb ik een vergadering,
maar vanmiddag kan ik wel even bij je langskomen

this morning I've got a meeting,
but this afternoon I can drop by and see you

de man met de hoed bedoel ik niet
dáár staat hij (lesson 7, 1.33–34)

the man with the hat is not the one I mean
there he is

altijd kom ik om zes uur thuis,
behalve op vrijdag

I always come home at 6 o'clock,
except on Friday

3   FURTHER REMARKS

(1.2) *kan ik u helpen?*   can I help you?
(1.3) *een boek over Amsterdam*   a book about Amsterdam
(1.10) *een ogenblikje, alstublieft* just a moment, please
(1.22) *de nummers staan op de boeken* the numbers are on the books
(1.33) *hier is nog zo'n boek*   here's a similar book
(1.39) **jawel,** *hier staat uw boek* yes I can, here's your book

(1.43) *jazeker, meneer*	certainly, Sir
(1.45) *komt u maar mee*	will you follow me?
(1.46) *kijkt u eens*	here you are
(1.53) *even kijken*	let's see
(1.52) *kan ik dit boek lenen?*	may I borrow this book?
iets lenen van iemand	to borrow something from somebody
iets lenen aan iemand (uitlenen)	to lend something out to somebody
die kunnen we niet uitlenen (1.59)	we can't lend those out
(1.61) *tot hoe laat bent u open?*	until what time are you open?
open zijn	to be open
open gaan (1.64)	to open up
dicht zijn	to be closed
dicht gaan	to close (down)
(1.66) *is dat elke avond zo?*	does that go for all evenings?

Elk(e) means 'each', 'every'
Elk is used before *het*-words: *elk boek*
Elke is used before *de*-words: *elke dag*
(cf. *welk(e)*, lesson 6, section 2.1)

(1.67-71) the days of the week:

zondag	Sunday
maandag	Monday
dinsdag	Tuesday
woensdag	Wednesday
donderdag	Thursday
vrijdag	Friday
zaterdag	Saturday

(see lesson 9, E. 8, 14, 15)

LESSON 9

1 SUMMARY OF THE DIALOGUE

After a lecture, Anneke asks Kees if she may borrow some of his notes. Then they go and have a cup of coffee. Anneke finds that she has lost her purse; she searches for it but it isn't there. Before she goes to the police, she intends looking at home. Kees and John have made an arrangement for the following Saturday to have dinner at Kees', and Kees now invites Anneke and her sister, Marianne, too.

Pay attention to the personal pronoun in subject and object function.

2 GRAMMAR

2.1 PERSONAL PRONOUNS
2.1.1 Forms used in object function

In this lesson the personal pronouns in object function are presented. Subject and object personal pronouns are given in the table below.

person		subject form without stress	subject form with stress	object form without stress	object form with stress
singular:	1	ik	ik	me	mij
	2 (informal)	je	jij	je	jou
	(formal)	u	u	u	u
	3	hij	hij	hem /əm/	hem
		ze	zij	haar /ər/, /dər/	haar
		het /ət/	het	het /ət/	het
plural:	1	we	wij	ons	ons
	2 (informal)	jullie	jullie	jullie	jullie
	(formal)	u	u	u	u
	3	ze	zij	ze (hen, hun)	– (die, hen, hun)

2.1.2 Functions of the object pronoun   E. 6–12

1. The pronoun as direct object

*zeg, is John ziek? ik zie **hem** nooit meer*
                    (line 31–32)

hey, is John ill? I don't see him around anymore

heb jij het collegedictaat van gisteren?
*ja, ik heb **het** bij me* (1.1–2)

have you got yesterday's lecture notes?
yes, I have them with me

ik heb mijn portemonnee altijd in mijn tasje,
*maar nu kan ik **hem** niet vinden*

I've always got my purse in my handbag,
but now I can't find it

*Anneke kan **mij** niet zien,*
*maar ik kan **haar** wel zien*

Anneke can't see me,
but I can see her

2. The pronoun as indirect object

*kan je **me** de wijn even geven?*   could you pass me the wine?

zou je zusje ook zin hebben?   might your sister like to come too?
*ik zal het **haar** vragen*   I'll ask her

3. The pronoun as prepositional object   **E. 14, 15**

*zaterdag komt hij bij **me** eten* (1.34)   on Saturday he's coming to dinner at my place
*bij **mij** op de hoek verkopen ze kip* (1.44)   in the shop at the corner of my street they sell chicken

*mag ik het van **je** lenen?* (1.4)   can I borrow it from you?
*morgen betaal ik wel voor **jou*** (1.63)   tomorrow I'll pay for you

2.1.3 The referents of the personal pronoun in the 3rd person   **E. 1–8, 10, 11**

Hij refers to:

1. one male person (subject)

***John** is niet ziek maar **hij** heeft het erg druk*   John isn't ill but he's very busy

2. singular *de*-words (subject)

*ik kan **mijn portemonnee** niet vinden*   I can't find my purse
*misschien ligt **hij** thuis*   perhaps it's at home

Hem refers to:

1. one male person (object of the sentence or following a preposition)

*zeg, is **John** ziek? ik zie **hem** nooit meer*   hey, is John ill? I don't see him around
(1.31–32)   anymore

2. a *de*-word (object of the sentence)

*ik kan **mijn portemonnee** niet vinden*   I can't find my purse
*heb jij **hem** niet in je jaszak?*   haven't you got it in your coat pocket?

Ze refers to:

1. one female person (subject of the sentence)

*dat is **mijn dochter, ze** studeert Engels*   that's my daughter, she studies English

2. two or more persons (subject or object of the sentence or following a preposition), as in

***Jaap en Els** gaan naar Rotterdam*   Jaap and Els go to Rotterdam
ze (subject) *missen de trein niet*   they don't miss the train
*Kees ontmoet **ze*** (direct object) *op*   Kees meets them at
*het station en praat **met ze***   the station and talks to them

3. two or more things (subject or object of the sentence)

dan liggen ze 's avonds voor me klaar (1.71)   then they are ready for me in the evening
en kan ik ze (object) *zo afhalen, met*   and I can fetch them together with
               de patat (1.72)   the chips

Hun and *hen* refer to two or more humans. The use of *hen* is restricted to a non-colloquial style. It mainly occurs in written language. In standard Dutch *hun* has the indirect object function and *hen* is used as direct object and prepositional object.

*John King vindt **zijn buren** heel aardig*   John King likes his neighbours a lot
*hij geeft **hun** dikwijls een bos bloemen*   he often gives them a bunch of flowers
*dan gaat hij even bij **hen** langs*   then he often drops by
*en praat met **hen***   and chats with them
*natuurlijk helpt hij **hen** altijd*   of course he always helps them

In colloquial Dutch one would use *ze* in all these four cases.

Haar refers to one female person (object of the sentence or after a preposition).

*is **Anneke** ziek? ik zie **haar** nooit meer*   is Anneke ill? I don't see her around any more

Het refers to:

1. a *het*-word (subject or object of the sentence)

*heb jij **het collegedictaat** van gisteren?* (1.1)   have you got yesterday's lecture notes?
*mag ik **het** van je lenen?* (1.3)   can I borrow them from you?
*natuurlijk, maar **het** is niet erg netjes* (1.4) of course, but they're not very neat

2. the content of the previous sentence/clause

nou, meestal kookt mijn moeder,   well, usually my mother cooks,
*maar in het weekend doe ik **het** wel eens* but at the weekends I do it occasionally
               (1.55–56)
zou je zusje ook zin hebben? (1.39)   might your sister like to come too?
*ik zal **het** haar vragen* (1.41)   I'll ask her

Het is usually pronounced /ət/ and is never stressed. If stress is necessary, *het* is replaced by *dat*.
o, bedoel je dat?   oh, is that what you mean?

N.B. *Het* is either a definite article before a *het*-word, as in (1.1) in the dialogue, or a pronoun, as in 1.3 and 1.4.

2.2 WORD ORDER: DIRECT AND INDIRECT OBJECT

The indirect object without preposition comes **before** the direct object (a).
The indirect object comes **after** the direct object if:
– the direct object is a personal pronoun (b)
– the indirect object is preceded by a preposition (c)

	indirect object	direct object	indirect object (+ preposition)
(a) *ik geef*	*het meisje*	*het boek*	
(c) *ik geef*		*het boek*	*aan het meisje*
(a) *ik geef*	*haar*	*het boek*	
(c) *ik geef*		*het boek*	*aan haar*
(b) *ik geef*		*het*	*haar*
(c) *ik geef*		*het*	*aan haar*

I give	the girl	the book	
I give		the book	to the girl
I give	her	the book	
I give		the book	to her
I give		it	her
I give		it	to her

2.3 VERBS
2.3.1 *Zullen* + infinitive and *gaan* + infinitive

Dutch has no separate form for indicating future time. For reference to the future we usually use the present tense:

ik betaal morgen wel voor jou (1.63)   tomorrow I'll pay for you

Gaan + infinitive and *zullen* + infinitive may also express an act or event in the future but if they do there is always a modal aspect involved.

***Gaan* + infinitive** expresses: ->

1. intention or plan, as in:

ga jij nog koffiedrinken? (1.11)   are you going to have coffee?

2. commencement of an act, as in:

ga maar vast zitten (1.29)   take a seat in the meantime
  Ik ga beginnen   I'm soj to start
***Zullen* + infinitive** expresses among other things:

1. a promise, or positive assurance, mostly in the 1st person, as in:

ik zal eerst thuis kijken (1.27)   I'll look for it at home first
ik zal het haar vragen (1.41)   I'll ask her

55

2. a suggestion or proposal, most often in a question sentence with a subject in the 1st person, as in:

zal ik dat even doen?   shall I do that?
(see lesson 10, E. 8, 9, 12)

2.3.2 *Zullen*

The present tense of *zullen* has irregular forms in the singular; the plural is regular.

ik   *zal*
je   *zult, zul je* (*je zal, zal je* also occurs)
u   *zult* (*u zal* also occurs)
hij   *zal*
ze   *zal*
het   *zal*
we   *zullen*
jullie zullen
u   *zult* (*u zal* also occurs)
ze   *zullen*

3 FURTHER REMARKS

3.1 *VAST*

The adverb *vast* (there is also an adjective *vast*) means:
1. 'meanwhile', 'in the meantime' (unstressed)

ga maar vast zitten   go and sit down in the meantime
ik haal de koffie wel (1.29–30)   I'll fetch the coffee

begint u maar vast. ik kom zo   just begin (in the meantime). I'll be there
                                              in a minute
wilt u al vast een kopje koffie   would you like a cup of coffee
voor we beginnen?   before we begin?

2. 'most likely'. In this meaning *vast* bears stress and expresses a strong belief or assumption on the part of the speaker.

John is vást ziek   John is most likely ill
John is vást niet ziek   I bet John is not ill
u bent vást een buitenlander   I bet you're a foreigner
je portemonnee zit vást in je jaszak   your purse is most likely in your coat pocket

3.2 *TOCH*

ik gebruik het tóch niet (1.10)	I won't be using it anyway

One of the several meanings of stressed *toch* is that it reinforces the positive or negative force of a contrastive statement:

ik heb geen paraplu bij me	I don't have an umbrella with me
want het regent tóch niet	because it isn't raining anyway
neem maar geen jas mee	don't bother taking a coat with you
want we gaan tóch met de auto	because we're going in the car (anyway)

3.3 MISCELLANEOUS REMARKS

(1.1) *zeg Kees, heb jij het collegedictaat van gisteren?* hey Kees, have you got yesterday's lecture notes?

Zeg is used here to draw Kees' attention (see also lesson 7, 1.30).

(1.9) *je mag het gerust de hele week houden* you can keep it all week, that's quite all right by me

(1.14) *dan kan het nog wel even* then I have some time left

(1.20) *daar heb ik hem nooit* I never keep it there

(1.37) *nee, ik heb nog niets* no, I haven't got anything yet

iets	something	*niets*	nothing
iemand	somebody	*niemand*	nobody
ergens	somewhere	*nergens*	nowhere
ooit	ever	*nooit*	never

(1.33) *hij heeft het erg druk* he is very busy

the fixed expression is: *het druk hebben*

cf. *het warm hebben*	to be/feel hot
het koud hebben	to be/feel cold

(1.35) *weet je wat, kom jij dan ook* you know what, why don't you come too?

weet je wat is an idiomatic expression introducing a spontaneous proposal. It is derived from:

weet je wat leuk is?	do you know what would be fun?
weet je wat we doen?	do you know what we'll do?

(1.39) *zou je zusje ook zin hebben?* might your sister like to come too?

(1.40) *dan zijn we met z'n vieren* that will make four of us

The construction *met* + *zijn* + numeral + *-en* indicates the number of persons.

ze komen met z'n vieren	there will be four of them
komen jullie met z'n vieren?	are there going to be four of you coming?

(1.45) *bij mij op de hoek verkopen ze kip aan het spit en patat* in the shop at the corner of my street they sell roast chicken and chips

(1.46) *ik zorg nog voor een schaal sla* and I'll make a salad
zorgen voor (E. 13) to take care, to see to it that something is done

(1.47) *en klaar is Kees* and there you are!

(1.49) *dan gaan we na het eten de stad **in***   then after dinner we'll go into town
Some prepositions may also be placed behind the nouns to which they belong. In such cases the notion of 'movement', 'direction' is involved.

*we wonen **op** de Hoofdweg*	we live on the Hoofdweg
*we gaan de Hoofdweg **op***	we're going to the Hoofdweg
*we zijn **in** de stad*	we're in town
*we gaan de stad **in***	we're going into town

(1.50) *naar een film **of zo***   to a film or something

(1.54) *kook jij eigenlijk vaak zelf?*   by the way, do you often do the cooking
                      yourself?

(1.60) *het eten is **er** wel niet zo lekker*   the food isn't really very good there
Er is an unstressed form of *daar.*

(1.64) *dat hoeft niet, hoor*   oh, there's no need

(1.61) *kom maar om een uur **of** vijf*   come about five o'clock
    *een uur **of** half zes*   about half past five
    *een minuut **of** tien*   about ten minutes
    *een week **of** drie*   about three weeks
    *een jaar **of** twee*   about two years

(1.69) *daarna moet ik even weg*   then I've got to go out quickly
    om het eten te halen   and fetch our dinner

He doe me denke aan
Il reminds me of

LESSON 10

1 SUMMARY OF THE DIALOGUE

Mrs Bergsma visits her father, who has been ill for five days. Fortunately, he has had some visitors during this time, and he has read a lot. Mrs Bergsma does the shopping and cooks dinner. Then they have dinner together. She says that she and the whole of her family have been to Amsterdam. While they were there, they called on Kees. At Kees' they met John King.

Pay attention to sentences with: PV*zijn* + past participle
PV*hebben*

This is the **perfect** (a past tense).

2 GRAMMAR

2.1 THE PERFECT TENSE
E. 1–7, 9–12, 16, 17

2.1.1 In this lesson we treat a verbal form which is used to indicate events or acts which took place in the past.

For speaking about the past, Dutch has **two** verbal forms:
1. perfect: treated in this lesson
2. simple past: to be treated in lesson 20

The perfect is used more often than the simple past. How these two forms differ from each other in use will be dealt with in lesson 20.

The formal structure of the perfect is:

PV (present) of *hebben* or *zijn* + past participle

Hebben and *zijn* have the function of auxiliaries to the past participle. The past participle always remains unchanged, regardless of the number etc. of the subject. For example:

ik ben   ziek geweest (I have been ill)
hij is   ziek geweest
we zijn ziek geweest

2.1.2 How to form the past participle

The past participle is not formed in the same way for all verbs. There are three types of verbs: weak, strong and irregular.

2.1.2.1 'Weak' verbs

Weak verbs form their past participle in the following way:

ge + stem + $\begin{array}{c} t \\ d \end{array}$

LESSON 10

More detailed information can be found in appendix B2.
The construction ends in -*t* if the stem ends in *p, t, k, s, f, ch.*
Some examples:

ik werk	*ik heb gewerkt*
ik kook	*ik heb gekookt*
ik praat	*ik heb gepraat*
ik woon	*ik heb gewoond*
ik leen	*ik heb geleend*
ik studeer	*ik heb gestudeerd*
ik speel	*ik heb gespeeld*

2.1.2.2 'Strong' verbs

The so-called 'strong' verbs (a relatively small group) form their past participle in a different way, and not according to one particular rule. The best policy is to learn the strong verbs by heart. More detailed information can be found in appendix B2.
Some examples:

ik lees	*ik heb gelezen*
ik zie	*ik heb gezien*
ik doe	*ik heb gedaan*
ik eet	*ik heb gegeten*
ik vind	*ik heb gevonden*
ik spreek	*ik heb gesproken*
ik lig	*ik heb gelegen*

2.1.2.3 Irregular verbs

There is also a group of verbs with an irregular past participle. In this lesson we encounter the following examples:

infinitive	present tense	perfect tense
zijn	*ik ben*	*ik ben geweest* (E.5)
hebben	*ik heb*	*ik heb gehad* (E.4)
kopen	*ik koop*	*ik heb gekocht* (1.46)

N.B. Pay attention to the difference between:

ik heb rijst gekookt	I've boiled some rice
ik heb rijst gekocht	I've bought some rice

2.1.3 The auxiliaries of the perfect

The auxiliaries of the perfect are *hebben* and *zijn*. In most cases *hebben* is the auxiliary:

hebt u in bed gelegen? (line 16)	have you been in bed?
ik heb bezoek gehad (1.19)	I have had visitors
hebt u wel genoeg gegeten? (1.26)	have you had enough to eat?
wat hebben jullie daar gedaan? (1.42)	what did you do there?
wat heb je gekocht? (1.45)	what have you bought?

Some verbs have *zijn* as auxiliary. In this lesson only one instance occurs:

Ik ben geweest (I have been)
je bent geweest
etc.
More information can be found in appendix B2.

2.1.4 The word order of a sentence in the perfect

In lesson 8, section 2.3 we saw that in a sentence with a verb phrase consisting of the PV of an auxiliary + an infinitive, the latter comes at the end of the sentence.

*Hier **kunt** u rustig **lezen***	here you can read quietly
kunt** u mijn boek niet **vinden?	can't you find my book?

The perfect tense also involves a compound verb phrase, consisting of the PV of either *hebben* or *zijn* + a past participle. The past participle also comes at the end of the sentence. As is usual, the PV of the auxiliary takes up second position in a declarative sentence.

*we **hebben** gisteren al met Kees **gepraat***	we already talked to Kees yesterday
*gisteren **hebben** we al met Kees **gepraat***	

2.2 *ER*   E. 13, 14

When the subject of a sentence is indefinite, the word *er*, which is roughly equivalent to unstressed 'there' in English, is added to the sentence. *Er* assumes the normal position of the subject, immediately before the PV; if inversion takes place, it will immediately follow the PV.

er is geen brood, er is geen melk (1.32)	there's no bread, there's no milk
*is **er** melk in huis?*	is there any milk in the house?
er zijn geen eieren, er zijn geen aardappels (1.33)	there are no eggs, there are no potatoes
*vandaag is **er** wijn bij het eten*	today there's wine with the meal
*is **er** wijn bij het eten vandaag?*	
er is wijn bij het eten vandaag	
*nu zitten **er** tien studenten in de leeszaal*	now there are ten students in the reading room
***er** zitten nu tien studenten in de leeszaal*	
*zitten **er** nu tien studenten in de leeszaal?*	

If you leave out *er* the meaning of the sentence changes:

er spelen kinderen in de tuin	there are children playing in the garden
kinderen spelen altijd graag buiten	children always like playing outdoors
er wacht een journalist op u	there's a journalist waiting for you
een journalist moet ook in het weekend werken	a journalist has to work at weekends too
er is nog melk	there's still some milk
is er nog melk?	is there any milk left?
melk is wit	milk is white
is melk wit?	is milk white?

3   FURTHER REMARKS

3.1 *ZULK(E)* AND *ZO'N*

het is zulk slecht weer (1.4)   the weather is so bad

Zulk(e) is a demonstrative and means 'to such a degree', 'of such a type'.
It is equivalent to *zo'n* (*zo een*).
Zulk(*e*) is used with – non-count nouns
                         – plural nouns

zulke boeken	such books
zulke melk	such milk
zulk weer	such weather

Note that *zulk* precedes *het*-words and *zulke* precedes *de*-words.
Zo'n is used with singular count nouns:

zo'n tafel	such a table
zo'n huis	such a house
zo'n man	such a man

3.2 *ZEKER*

Zeker, stressed as well as unstressed, has many meanings. In one of its meanings unstressed *zeker* expresses a supposition of the speaker. The speaker supposes that something is the case but he is not sure.

*u bent vandaag **zeker** nog niet búiten geweest* (1.6)	you haven't been out today, I suppose? (rising intonation)
*en u hebt **zeker** veel gelézen?* (1.23)	and I suppose you've read a lot, haven't you?
*u wilt **zeker** naar béd?* (1.66)	you'll be wanting to go to bed I suppose?

3.3 *WEL*

In lesson 6, section 3 it was noted that stressed *wel* can express or reinforce the positive force of a statement, often in contrast with a previous statement, often in contrast with an implicit assumption, as in:

ik ben nu weer beter	I'm better now
maar ik moet nog wél binnen blijven	but I still have to stay indoors (though)
(1.13-14)	

In the following example, however, *wel* does not bear stress:

en hebt u wel genoeg gegeten? (1.26)	and have you eaten enough?

In this case Mevr. Bergsma uses *wel* to add force to her doubt whether the implied assertion that father did have enough to eat is positively true.

wilt u nu misschien iets eten?	would you like to eat something now perhaps?
ja, éigenlijk wél (1.28-29)	yes, I would actually (if you want me to give an honest although perhaps impolite answer, I would say 'yes, I do')

Unstressed *wel* may also express a willingness or promise on the part of the speaker to do something:

ik máák wel iets voor u (1.30)	I'll make something for you
ik ga wel even bóódschappen doen	I'll just go out and do some shopping
ik kom wel weer eens lángs	I'll drop by again some time

3.4 *TOCH*

Note the following examples with *toch*:

toch niet érg? (1.11)	nothing serious, I hope?
je bent toch niet ziék?	you're not ill, I hope?
je hebt je portemonnéé toch wel bij je?	you've got your purse with you, I hope?
de dokter is toch wel geweest?	the doctor has been, I hope?

3.5 MISCELLANEOUS REMARKS

(1.5)	*het stormt en het regent dat het giet*	it is stormy and it's raining cats and dogs
	het giet	it's raining very hard, it's pouring
	het regent dat het giet	the same meaning but stronger
	het giet van de regen	
(1.7)	*ik mag niet eens naar buiten*	I'm not even allowed out

LESSON 10

(1.36) *maar nu is alles op*
     op zijn:
     1. to be out, to be finished (see lesson 17, E. 2, 4)
     2. to be up, out of bed

ik was al vroeg op vanmorgen	I was up early this morning

     3. to be exhausted

na een dag werken ben je soms	after a day's work you are sometimes
(dood)op	(dead)tired
(1.37) *dan ga ik nu eerst even*	then I'll go and do some shopping quickly
boodschappen doen	
(1.40) *en vertel eens, hoe is het thuis?*	and tell me, how are things at home?
(1.48) *een paar sokken voor Hans*	

     een paar:
     1. a pair of

een paar sokken	a pair of socks
een paar schoenen	a pair of shoes

     2. some, a few

ik heb een paar boeken geleend	I've borrowed some books
(1.52) *Kees heeft hem vorig jaar*	Kees met him last year on the boat
op de boot ontmoet	

het	*jaar*	the year
de	*week*	the week
vorig	*jaar*	last year
vorige	*week*	last week
volgend	*jaar*	next year
volgende	*week*	next week

Ontmoet is the participle of *ontmoeten*. There is more about this type of past participle in lesson 12.

(1.65) *ik heb **veel te lang** gepraat*	I've been talking much too long

Te + adjective can be reinforced by putting *veel* before it. If the adjective is not preceded by *te* it is reinforced by means of *erg* (or *heel*).

ik heb te lang gepraat	I've talked too long
ik heb veel te lang gepraat	I've talked much too long
ik heb erg lang gepraat	I've talked very long
ik heb heel lang gepraat	I've talked very long

LESSON 11

1 SUMMARY OF THE DIALOGUE

Anneke and her mother go into town together. First they buy a shirt for Anneke's father in a menswear shop. Then they go to the post office: Anneke needs some stamps and wants to send a parcel to Norway, while her mother wants to withdraw *f* 100,– from her giro account.

Pay attention to adjectives preceding a noun: sometimes an adjective ends in -*e*, sometimes it does not.

2 GRAMMAR

2.1 THE ADJECTIVE
2.1.1 The adjective in combination with a noun   E. 1, 3, 5, 7, 9–13

The adjective can be used in two ways:

1. predicatively (following the subject and PV). In this use an -*e* is never added to the adjective.

de tafel is mooi	the table is beautiful
het huis is oud	the house is old

2. attributively (immediately preceding a noun). In this use, an -*e* is very often affixed to the adjective. Only in one case is there no such affix: if the adjective precedes a singular *het*-word and at the same time follows the words *een, geen, veel, weinig* etc.

***Het*-words**

singular definite	*het mooie huis*
indefinite	*een mooi huis*
plural definite	*de mooie huizen*
indefinite	*mooie huizen*

ik moet een nieuw overhemd voor vader hebben (line 4)	I must have a new shirt for father
hier hebben we de witte overhemden (1.20)	here are the white shirts
veel helder water	much clear water
weinig helder water	little clear water

LESSON 11

De-words:

singular	definite	*de mooie tafel*
	indefinite	*een mooie tafel*
plural	definite	*de mooie tafels*
	indefinite	*mooie tafels*

hier heb je een goede winkel voor herenkleding (1.13)   here's a good shop for menswear

Pay attention to the spelling of the adjective:

een geel huis	*een rood huis*	*een wit huis*
het gele huis	*het rode huis*	*het witte huis*
gele huizen	*rode huizen*	*witte huizen*
de gele huizen	*de rode huizen*	*de witte huizen*

2.1.2 Adjectives without a noun   E. 2, 4, 6, 8, 14

In some cases the noun is not realized because it has been mentioned earlier. The 'lonely' adjective which remains keeps strictly to the normal rules for adjectives. In English such an adjective would be accompanied by the 'prop word' **one**, but Dutch doesn't have such a prop word.

waarom neemt u geen groen overhemd of een geel? (1.28)   why don't you take a green shirt or a yellow one?

ik neem het witte (1.33)   I'll take the white one

wat een vrolijke! (kinderzegels) (1.50)   how nice and cheerful! (child welfare stamps)

geeft u me maar vijf kinderzegels en vijf gewone (1.51)   give me five childrens' stamps and five ordinary ones

2.1.3 Undeclined adjectives

There are a number of adjectives to which the suffix *-e* is never added:

1. adjectives ending in *-en: gouden* ('gold'), *open* ('open'), *gesloten* ('closed')

een gouden ketting   a gold chain
de open deur   the open door

2. some names of colours and materials: *lila* ('lilac'), *plastic* ('plastic'), *nylon* ('nylon'), *beige* ('beige'), *oranje* ('orange')

het nylon overhemd   the nylon shirt

3. adjectives in *-er* denoting placenames: *Groninger, Deventer*

Groninger koek   gingerbread (from Groningen)
Deventer koek   gingerbread (from Deventer)

66

4. *rechter* and *linker*

de rechter hand	the right hand
de linker hand	the left hand

2.2 VERBS
2.2.1 *Zal ik, zullen we* E. 18

The 1st person singular and plural of *zullen* + infinitive can be used in a question sentence to make a proposal:

zal ik komen?	shall I come?
zullen we even naar binnen gaan? (1.14)	shall we go in?

N.B. In a declarative sentence *zullen* may express a promise, as in:
  ik zal het morgen vragen   I'll ask tomorrow

2.2.2 *Laten we* E. 16

1. The 1st person plural of *laten* + infinitive (in the word order of the question sentence) denotes a strong suggestion or wish on the part of the speaker.

laten we gaan	let's go
laten we de rest morgen maar doen	let's do the rest tomorrow

2. *Laten we* is also used in answer to the proposal *zullen we?*

zullen we even naar binnen gaan?	shall we go in?
ja, laten we hier maar eens gaan kijken	yes, let's have a look around

3 FURTHER REMARKS

3.1 *SOMS*

Soms can be used in three different senses in Dutch.

1. Stressed *soms* means 'sometimes'.

sóms werk ik overdag	sometimes I work in the daytime
en sóms werk ik 's nachts	and sometimes I work at night

2. Unstressed *soms* can be used in a question to make the request less straightforward, less direct, more friendly. One can often substitute *soms* for *misschien*.

ga je soms méé? (1.2)	do you want to come along perhaps?
heb je soms zin om méé te gaan?	do you possibly fancy coming along?
heb je misschien zin om méé te gaan?	do you possibly fancy coming along?
wil je soms een kopje kóffie?	would you like a cup of coffee perhaps?

LESSON 11

3. In a question sentence unstressed *soms* can also be used to add force to an assumption the speaker has.

ben je soms ziek?	are you ill by any chance?
zal ik de dokter bellen?	shall I phone the doctor?
heb je soms geen geld?	have you got no money by any chance?
moet je wat van mij hebben?	do you want to borrow some?
ga je soms met de auto?	you don't happen to be going in the car, do you?
mag ik dan mee?	can I have a lift if you are?

3.2 WAT

Wat often occurs at the beginning of an exclamation. Note the following examples:

wat een vrolijke (1.50)	how nice and cheerful!
wat is het hier druk (1.61)	it's busy here, isn't it?
wat een mooie jas	what a nice coat
wat een mooie jassen	what nice coats
wat een mooi boek	what a nice book
wat een mooie boeken	what nice books

3.3 MISCELLANEOUS REMARKS

(1.6) *dat zegt hij **tenminste***	so he says at any rate
(1.29) *dat is **tenminste** modern*	at least that's modern
(1.11) *o, ik heb postzegels nodig*	oh, I need stamps
(1.12) *dan kan ik die **gelijk** kopen*	then I can buy them at the same time
(1.13) *hier **heb je** een goede winkel voor herenkleding*	here's a good shop for menswear
(1.20) *hier **hebben we** de witte overhemden*	here are the white shirts
(1.23) *wat vind je van dit overhemd?*	what about this shirt?
(1.27) *moet het nou echt wit zijn?*	well, must it really be white?

For the names of colours, see the supplementary glossary on page 85 in the course book.

(1.35) *wenst u **verder** nog iets?*	is there anything else/further you want?

Here *verder* means 'in addition to'

*Parijs is **verder dan** Brussel*	Paris is further than Brussels

Note that *verder* in Dutch thus has both the meanings of 'further' in English.

(1.38) *die is **beneden***	that's downstairs

When the adverbs *buiten, binnen, beneden, boven* are used to indicate the direction of a movement they are preceded by *naar*:

ik ben binnen	I'm inside
ik ga naar binnen	I'm going in(side)
ik ben buiten	I'm outside .
ik ga naar buiten	I'm going out(side)
hij is boven	he's upstairs

68

hij gaat naar boven	he's going upstairs
hij is beneden	he's downstairs
hij gaat naar beneden (E. 17)	he's going downstairs

N.B. If the verb is *komen, naar* is optional:

ik kom beneden	I'm coming downstairs
ik kom naar beneden	

(1.45)	*zegt u het maar, juffrouw*	what can I do for you? can I help you?
(1.49)	*maar die hebben een **flinke** toeslag*	but they're quite a bit more expensive

Here *flinke* has the sense of 'considerable'.

	But: *een flinke jongen*	a big boy (physical size); a brave boy
(1.52)	*en ik wou deze pakjes versturen*	and I would like to send these small parcels
(1.57)	*enzovoorts (enz.)*	etcetera (etc.)
(1.59)	*met f 1,30*	and f 1,30 change
(1.63)	*maar nu ben ik bijna aan de beurt*	but now it's almost my turn

LESSON 12

1 SUMMARY OF THE DIALOGUE

John and Kees happen to see each other in the Valeriusstraat; they're both on their way to the same wedding reception. Kees explains the proceedings at a Dutch wedding reception. At the reception they have a chat with Mrs Van Mierlo about the bride and her family and Mrs Van Mierlo's daughter-in-law, who is also English.

Pay attention to: – forms of the perfect
- *waar, waarnaartoe, waarvandaan*
- how one congratulates someone and how one introduces people to each other

2 GRAMMAR

2.1 VERBS WITH AN UNSTRESSED PREFIX E. 3, 6

The past participle of verbs with one of the following unstressed prefixes does not take the prefix *ge-: be-, her-, ver-, er-, ont-, ge-.*
Note these examples:

ontmoeten	*hij heeft ontmoet*	to meet
vertellen	*hij heeft verteld*	to tell
herhalen	*hij heeft herhaald*	to repeat
beginnen	*hij is begonnen*	to begin
gebruiken	*hij heeft gebruikt*	to use
verhuizen	*hij is verhuisd*	to move house

There will be more verbs with an unstressed prefix treated in lesson 13.

2.2 THE AUXILIARY *ZIJN* E. 4

All intransitive verbs which express a change in condition or location take *zijn* as auxiliary in the perfect tense. In this lesson we see a number of verbs of this kind: *gaan, komen, verhuizen, vertrekken* (to leave), *beginnen, blijven.*

2.3 QUESTION WORDS AND THE CORRESPONDING DEMONSTRATIVES
2.3.1 *Waar, waarnaartoe, waarvandaan*

Waar ('where') is a question word asking for the place of something:

waar is het postkantoor? where is the post office?

Waarnaartoe ('where (to)') is a question word asking for the direction or the goal of a movement:

hallo John, waar ga jij naar toe? (line 1)   hallo, John, where are you going?

Waarvandaan ('where from', 'from where') asks for the starting point of a movement:
waar komen jullie vandaan?   where do you come from? (i.e. where do you live/what is your home town?)

waar komen jullie net vandaan?   where have you just come from?

Waarnaartoe and *waarvandaan* are usually split up in two parts. *Waar* takes the first position in the sentence, *vandaan* and *naartoe* the last or next to last:

waar *ga je nu* **naartoe?**
waar *ben je gisteravond* **naartoe** *geweest?*
waar *kom je nu* **vandaan?**
waar *ben je gisteren* **vandaan** *gekomen?*

2.3.2 *Daar, daarnaartoe, daarvandaan*   E. 7, 8

Daar ('there') is the demonstrative corresponding with *waar:*

kijk, daar staat het bruidspaar (1.24)   look, there's the bridal couple

Daarnaartoe ('there') corresponds with *waarnaartoe:*

daar ga ik ook naartoe (1.2)   I'm going there too

Daarnaartoe and *daarvandaan* are also split up:

daar *ga ik ook* **naartoe**
daar *ben ik gisteravond ook* **naartoe** *geweest*
daar *kom ik* **vandaan**
daar *ben ik net* **vandaan** *gekomen*

N.B. *John komt* **uit** *Engeland*   John's from England
    daar kom ik ook vandaan   that's where I'm from, too

    John komt **van** *de receptie*   John has come from the reception
    daar kom ik ook vandaan   that's where I've come from, too

ik kom uit Engeland can have two meanings:

1. I live there/have lived there/was born there
2. I have just arrived from England

2.4 *BEDOELEN, BETEKENEN, MENEN*

bedoelen: 1. 'to mean', 'try to say something'

wat bedoelt u?	what are you trying to say? what do you mean?

2. 'try to point out'

ik bedoel die man met de rode hoed I mean that man with the red hat

Bedoelen always has a subject referring to a human being.

bedoeling: 'what you intend to say or try to point out'

is dat je bedoeling?	is that what you mean?

betekenen: 'to symbolize', 'to stand for'

wat betekenen de letters A.O.W.?	What do the letters A.O.W. mean?
dat betekent	they stand for
Algemene Ouderdoms Wet	'Algemene Ouderdoms Wet'

betekenis: 'meaning', 'that which is symbolized'

dat is de betekenis van de drie letters	that's the meaning of the three letters
wat is de betekenis van dat woord?	what's the meaning of that word?

menen: 1. 'to think that', 'to be of the opinion that'

ik meen dat hij rookt	I think that he smokes

2. 'to mean', 'to be serious'

meen je dat echt?	do you really mean that?

mening: 'opinion'

mijn mening vragen ze niet	they don't ask for my opinion

2.5 DEZELFDE, HETZELFDE

Dezelfde and *hetzelfde* mean 'the same'.
Dezelfde is used before *de*-words and plural nouns.
Hetzelfde is used before singular *het*-words.

Kees en John gaan naar dezelfde receptie	Kees and John are going to the same reception
Anneke en Kees kopen hetzelfde boek	Anneke and Kees buy the same book
hebben Kees en John dezelfde vrienden?	do Kees and John have the same friends?

Dezelfde and *hetzelfde* may also occur independently:

koop jij een ander boek?	are you going to buy another book?
nee, ik koop hetzelfde	no, I'm going to buy the same one

N.B. *Hetzelfde* can also mean 'the same thing':

'vlakbij' betekent hetzelfde als *'dichtbij'*	*'vlak bij'* means the same thing as *'dichtbij'*
een fiets en een bromfiets, *dat is niet hetzelfde*	a bike and a moped, that's not the same thing

2.6 *TOEN*

The adverb *toen* has two meanings:

1. 'then', 'at that moment'

toen ben ik naar huis gegaan	then I went home

2. 'after that' in the past

ze hebben eerst drie jaar in Engeland gewoond	first they lived in England for three years
en toen zijn ze naar Rotterdam gegaan (1.67)	and then they went to Rotterdam

N.B. 'After that', 'then' when used to refer to present and future is in Dutch *dan*.

eerst gaan we naar Amsterdam *en dan naar Den Haag*	first we're going to Amsterdam and then to The Hague

Further information on *toen* and *dan* can be found in lesson 21, section 2.3.

2.7 INTRODUCING PEOPLE TO EACH OTHER

In highly formal situations, the introducing of people follows a fixed procedure.

2.7.1 Two people being introduced to each other by a third

Person A says to person B:

mag ik C aan u voorstellen? or *mag ik u voorstellen: dit is C*	I'd like you to meet Mr C

Then he says to Mr/Mrs C:

dit is meneer/mevrouw B	this is Mr/Mrs B

then B and C shake hands and say:

hoe maakt u het? (see dialogue 1.33–36)	how do you do?

LESSON 12

Hoe maakt u het? has fallen into almost complete disuse. If anything at all, one would probably say *dag meneer/mevrouw.*

N.B. The expression *hoe gaat het met u/je?* is not used when you meet someone for the first time, but only when you meet someone you are acquainted with (cf. lesson 3, section 3.1).

2.7.2 Two persons make acquaintance without a third person present

One of them says:

we hebben nog geen kennis gemaakt or   we haven't met yet
ik wilde graag met u kennis maken or   I would like to make acquaintance with you
mag ik me even voorstellen?   may I introduce myself?

Then they say in turn:

ik ben . . . or   I am . . .
mijn naam is . . .   my name is . . .

Then they shake hands.

3 FURTHER REMARKS

(1.5) **een vriend van mij** *trouwt vandaag*   a friend of mine is getting married today
You can use the possessive pronoun in order to express that you possess (in a very wide sense) someone or something. But beside this, you can also use the construction:
van + object
Kees heeft een vriend, dat is zijn vriend   (that's his friend)
                dat is een vriend van Kees   (that's a friend of Kees')
If the pronoun is used, it takes the object form:
                dat is een vriend van hem   (that's a friend of his)
(lesson 13, E. 8)

(1.12) *je vriend ken ik pas kort*   I've met your friend only recently
     (E. 13)

(1.13) *ik heb hem twee dagen geleden*   I met him for the first time
             voor het eerst ontmoet   two days ago
     twee dagen geleden   two days ago
     over twee dagen   in two days
     cf. (1.47) *drie jaar geleden*   three years ago
     voor het eerst   for the first time

(1.20) *je zegt gewoon*   you just say
             'hartelijk gefeliciteerd'   'congratulations'
     gewoon (adverb)   just

gewoon (adjective)	common, usual
gewoonlijk	usually

(1.26) *van harte gefeliciteerd*   best congratulations
           met je huwelijk   on your wedding

van harte gefeliciteerd
hartelijk gefeliciteerd
wel   *gefeliciteerd*

hartelijk gefeliciteerd   many happy returns
         met je verjaardag

wel gefeliciteerd met je examen   congratulations on passing your exam
(E. 9)

The person who has been congratulated replies: *dank je wel/dank u wel*

(1.32) *en ik een borrel graag*   and a jenever for me, please

Jenever is kind of Dutch gin, flavoured with juniper berries.

(1.37) *wat ziet de bruid er mooi uit, hè?*   doesn't the bride look beautiful?

     1. *er* + adjective + *uitzien*   to look + adjective
        er   *mooi*   *uitzien*   to look   beautiful
     2. *er uitzien als* + number   to look + number
        er uitzien als   *16* (1.43)   to look   16
     3. *er uitzien als* + noun   to look like + noun
        er uitzien als   *een geest*   to look like   a ghost
     (E. 11)

(1.42) *dat zou je niet zeggen*   you wouldn't think so (literally: you
                                         wouldn't say that)

(1.54) *nee toch!*   you don't, do you?

See also lesson 5, section 3.4 and lesson 10, section 3.4.

(1.60) *A.O.W.*

This is a state pension received by every person in the Netherlands from the age of 65 onwards regardless of their income.

aan je A.O.W. toe zijn   to become 65, to be almost 65

(1.71) *maar ze is nog lang niet zover als u* but she isn't by far so advanced as you are
ver:

     1. a) a certain distance
     hoe ver is het van Amsterdam naar   how far is it from Amsterdam to
                 Utrecht?   Utrecht?
       b) a great distance
       dat is heel ver   that's very far
     2. 'to be advanced', 'to have progressed'
     ze is al ver met Nederlands   her Dutch has already progressed a lot

LESSON 12

(1.72)	*ze doet haar best*	she does her best
	ik doe mijn best	I do my best
	etc.	
(1.26)	*huwelijk*	marriage, wedding
(1.6)	*receptie*	reception
(1.14)	*bruiloft*	wedding

For *schoonvader, schoonmoeder* etc. see the supplementary glossary on page 93 of the course book.

LESSON 13

1 SUMMARY OF THE DIALOGUE

Anneke and Kees agree to go to a film. Kees phones up to reserve seats. He's going to borrow a moped to fetch Anneke, because he has sold his own moped. On arriving home, Anneke is told that John has phoned: he wants to invite her to a party.

Pay attention to – *er* in, for instance: *ik heb er nog twee*

een vriend van me heeft er een

– compounds verbs

2 GRAMMAR

2.1 *ER*

In this lesson *er* occurs in combination with *(g)een, twee, drie, veel, weinig, genoeg* etc. In the second example below, for instance, *er geeneen* can be said to be a pronominal form of *geeneen kwartje*.

heb jij misschien **een kwartje** *voor me?* (line 20)	have you got 25 cents for me perhaps?
ik heb **er geeneen** *meer* (1.22)	I haven't got a single one left
ik heb **er** *nog* **twee** (1.34)	I've got two
ik wil **een bandrecorder** *hebben* (1.44)	I want a tape recorder
een vriend van mij heeft **er een** (1.45)	a friend of mine has one
weet jij hier ergens **een brievenbus?** (1.48)	do you know a post box anywhere around here?
er zijn **er twee** *in één straat* (1.49)	there's two of them in one street
en op het plein, daar is **er ook een** (1.52)	and on the square, there's one there too

Compare the above examples involving *er* with the examples below:

heb jij **het kaartje?**	have you got the ticket?
nee, ik heb **het** *niet, maar hij heeft* **het** *wel*	no, I haven't, but he's got it
heb jij **de kaartjes?**	have you got the tickets?
nee, ik heb **ze** *niet, maar hij heeft* **ze** *wel*	no, I haven't, but he's got them
bel je **een dokter** *op?* (E. 11)	will you phone a doctor?
ik heb **er** *al* **een** *opgebeld*	I've already phoned one
nee, ik heb **er geen** *opgebeld*	no, I haven't phoned one
bel je **de dokter** *op?*	will you phone the doctor?
ik heb **hem** *al opgebeld*	I've already phoned him
nee, ik heb **hem** *niet opgebeld*	no, I haven't phoned him

LESSON 13

In lesson 10 we saw that an indefinite subject can be supplemented by means of *er:*

er liggen vier boeken op tafel   there are four books on the table
er zijn twee brievenbussen in één straat there are two post boxes in one street

If, in these sentences, we want to use *er twee,* we get two *er*s in one sentence:

er liggen er twee op tafel   there are two of them on the table
er zijn er twee in één straat (1.49) there's two of them in one street

There is more information about *er* in Appendix D3.

2.2 COMPOUND VERBS

A compound verb is a verb consisting of a prefix and a verb. There are two types of compound verbs.

2.2.1 Compound verbs with an unstressed prefix (e.g. *ontmóéten* (see lesson 12))

When the verbs has an unstressed prefix, this prefix always remains attached to the stem and the past participle of the verb does not take *ge-*.

ontmóéten	(to meet)	*ik ontmóét een*	*Engelsman*	*ik heb een*	*Engelsman*	*ontmoet*
verkópen	(to sell)	*ik verkóóp mijn*	*fiets*	*ik heb mijn fiets*		*verkocht*
bespréken	(to reserve a seat)	*ik bespréék de*	*plaatsen*	*ik heb de*	*plaatsen*	*besproken*

2.2.2 Compound verbs with a stressed prefix (e.g. *ópbellen*)

In this lesson a number of verbs have stressed prefixes:

ópbellen	to telephone	*néérzetten*	to put down
áfhalen	to fetch	*úitstellen*	to postpone
lángskomen	to drop by	*ínvullen*	to fill in
úitnodigen	to invite	*vásthouden*	to hold
méénemen	to take with one	*ópschrijven*	to write down

In the present tense the prefix usually takes the last place in the sentence:

*ik **houd** hem wel even **vast*** (1.18)   I'll hold it
*ik **zet** hem hier wel **neer*** (1.19)   I'll put it here
neem** ze allebei maar **mee (1.28)   take them both
*hij **komt** vanavond even **langs*** (1.61)   he's dropping by tonight
*voor die tijd **bel** ik John nog wel even **op***   I'll call John before then
(1.71)

In the past participle *ge-* comes between the prefix and the verb stem:

op ge beld
uit ge nodigd
mee ge nomen
langs ge komen

John heeft net voor je opgebeld (1.60)	John's just phoned for you
dat hebben we uitgesteld tot 7 mei (1.66)	we've postponed that till 7 May

If *te* has to be supplied to the infinitive, it is put between the prefix and the verb stem:

*heb jij zin om **mee** te **gaan?*** (1.5)	do you fancy going too?
*heb jij misschien een kwartje voor me om **op** te **bellen?*** (1.20–21)	have you possibly got 25 cents for me so I can make a phone call?

infinitive + *te*	infinitive without *te*
... om ... op te bellen	*ik zal hem opbellen*
... om ... af te halen	*ik zal ze afhalen*
... om ... uit te nodigen	*ik zal haar uitnodigen*
... om ... langs te komen	*ik zal langskomen*

2.3 THE CONSTRUCTION *OM* + *TE* + INFINITIVE

The construction *om* + *te* + infinitive has many meanings and functions. In this lesson it occurs in the following ways:

1. purpose or goal

daarna moet ik even weg om het eten te halen	then I must go out quickly (in order) to fetch our dinner
Els gaat naar Rotterdam om de Picassotentoonstelling te zien	Els is going to Rotterdam to see the Picasso exhibition

2. function (following a noun)

een kwartje om op te bellen (1.20-21)	25 cents to make a telephone call

3: *hoelang duurt het om van jou naar de bioscoop te fietsen?* (1.36)	how long does it take to cycle from your place to the cinema?

4. *heb je zin om mee te gaan?* (1.5)	do you fancy going too?

LESSON 13

2.4 DATES

Indicating a date is done in the following, fixed order:
1. name of the day
2. number of the day
3. name of the month
4. the year

woensdag 19 februari 1975

The names of the days and months are not written with a capital letter. When dates or the names of the days are used as an adjunct of time, they are preceded by the preposition *op* (or by no preposition at all).

(op) maandag 24 augustus vertrekken we	we leave on Monday, 24 August
het feestje is (op) 22 april	the party is on 22 April

Before months and years the preposition is *in*:

in april ga ik naar Engeland	in April I'm going to England
ze zijn in 1974 verhuisd	they moved house in 1974

For the names of months, see the supplementary glossary on page 101 of the course book.

3 FURTHER REMARKS

3.1 *LINKS* AND *RECHTS*

linksaf (1.51)	to the left (direction of movement)
rechtsaf (1.54)	to the right
rechtdoor (1.55)	straight on
ik moet hier rechtsaf (1.54)	I have to go right here
links	left
aan je linker hand	on your left (hand)
rechts	right
aan je rechter hand	on your right (hand)

3.2 MISCELLANEOUS REMARKS

(1.4) *ik ga er vanavond naartoe*	I'm going to see it tonight
This use of *er* is explained in lesson 14.	
(1.6) *ik ga graag mee*	yes, I'd like to come
(1.8) *ja, ik geloof het wel*	yes, I think so
(1.19) *ach nee*	oh, no
(1.7) *hij **draait** in Kriterion*	it is on at the Kriterion

(1.27) *je kunt best een verkeerd nummer*   you may well dial a wrong number
              draaien

(1.22) *ik heb er geeneen meer*   I haven't got a single one left
       Geeneen means 'not anyone', 'not anything'. *Geeneen* is a stronger way of expressing
       geen.

(1.28) *neem ze allebei maar mee*   take them both

(1.47) *ik heb **net** een brief aan hem*   I've just written him a letter
              geschreven

(1.60) *John heeft **net** voor je opgebeld*   John tried to call you just now

LESSON 14

1 SUMMARY OF THE DIALOGUE

Kees, Jaap en Els talk about what was on TV the previous evening. Els watched an opera and Kees watched some motor cycle racing as he doesn't like operas. He finds all that singing unnatural. This evening they decide to watch a lecture and after that an organ concert. Unfortunately, the loudspeaker of the old television set appears to have broken down, so they have to make do with the picture.

Pay attention to: – *er*
– sentences witch a prepositional object
– sentences beginning with *als*

2 GRAMMAR

2.1 *ER, HIER, DAAR* AND *WAAR* AS PRONOMINAL OBJECTS OF PREPOSITIONS
2.1.1 Forms

In this lesson a number of verbs occur which do not take a direct object but a prepositional object. This means that the verb goes together with a fixed preposition, e.g. *luisteren naar,* which means 'to listen to', and the preposition is followed by the object (the prepositional object), e.g. *luisteren naar de radio,* which means 'to listen to the radio'. In the examples below the prepositions are printed in bold face and the prepositional objects follow them:

ik houd niet **van** opera	I don't like opera
ik kijk nooit **naar** motorraces	I never watch motor racing
we lachen **om** die gekke situatie	we're laughing about that crazy situation
we spelen nooit **met** vuur	we never play with fire
hij praat **over** zijn moeilijkheden	he's talking about his difficulties
hij heeft het **over** zijn moeilijkheden	he's talking about his difficulties
hij gaat **naar** een vergadering	he's going to a meeting
ze komt **uit** Engeland	she comes from England

To refer to a prepositional object which does not denote a human, we use the pronouns *er, hier, daar* and *waar,* words that, literally, denote place.

*heb je **daarnaar** gekeken?* (line 8)   did you watch it?
Here *daar* refers to *de motorraces in Assen.*
(*de*-word plural)
daar** houd ik nu helemaal niet **van (1.10)   that's something I don't like at all
Here *daar* refers to *dat geraas.*
(*het*-word singular)

*Els heeft **ernaar** gekeken* (1.18)	Els saw it

Here *er* refers to *de opera*.
(*de*-word singular)

*hij kan **er** alleen maar **om** lachen* (1.33)	he can only laugh at them

Here *er* refers to *opera's*
(*de*-word plural)

***daar** hoeven we niet **naar** te kijken* (1.39)	we don't have to see that

Here *daar* refers to *de film 'spelen met vuur'*.
(*de*-word singular)

daar** spelen we toch nooit **mee (1.40)	after all, it's something we never play with

Here *daar* refers to *vuur*.
(*het*-word singular)

*ik luister **er** nooit **naar*** (1.48)	I never listen to it

Here *er* refers to *orgelmuziek*.
(*de*-word singular)

waar** hebben jullie het **over? (1.12)	what are you talking about?
*een reportage, **waarvan?*** (1.6)	a report of what?
jullie hebben ook moeilijkheden, zie ik (1.60)	you've got problems as well, I see
***waarmee** dan?* (1.61)	what with then?
met jullie TV (1.62)	with your TV

As you can see from the examples above, *er, hier* and *daar* can refer to singular *de*-words, singular *het*-words, as well as plurals.

2.1.2 Meanings. The difference between *er* and *daar* + preposition

In lesson 8, section 2.1.2, it was noted that *die/dat* can refer to something already mentioned in the previous sentence, in order to establish a direct link with that topic (see also section 2.4 under 1. in lesson 8). One could conceive of the use of *die/dat* as the first pronominal reference to a new topic. The same is true for the meaning of *daar* + preposition. This is also illustrated in lesson 14, E. 10–12 for *daar* + preposition, and in lesson 8, E. 12 for *die/dat* in direct object function.

prepositional object:

*kijkt u wel eens naar **het televisiejournaal?***	do you ever watch the news on TV?
*nee, **daar** kijk ik nooit naar*	no, I never watch it
*luistert u wel eens naar **de radionieuwsdienst?***	do you ever listen to the news on the radio?
*nee, **daar** luister ik nooit naar*	no, I never listen to it
*praat u wel eens over **de moeilijkheden in onze economie?***	do you ever talk about the problems in our economy?
*nee, **daar** praat ik nooit over*	no, I never talk about them

LESSON 14

direct object:

*heb je **het televisiejournaal** gisteren gezien?*	did you see the news om TV yesterday?
*nee, **dat** heb ik niet gezien*	no, I didn't see it
*heb je **de radionieuwsdienst** om 8 uur gehoord?*	did you hear the news on the radio at 8 o'clock?
*nee, **die** heb ik niet gehoord*	no, I didn't hear it
*wat vind je van **de moeilijkheden** in de economie?*	what do you think of the problems in the economy?
***die** vind ik niet zo groot*	I don't think they're too great

When you want to refer to a topic which has not only been already mentioned but which has, for instance, been further referred to as well, you do so by means of the pronoun *er* + preposition (rather than *daar* + preposition), and *hem/het/ze* (rather than *die/dat*) in the case of a direct object.

prepositional object:

het televisiejournaal?	the news on TV?
*nee hoor, **daar** kijk ik nooit naar*	oh no, I never watch it
maar mijn vrouw wel	but my wife does
*die kijkt **er** elke avond naar*	she watches it every night
de radionieuwsdienst?	the news on the radio?
*ja, **daar** luister ik elke morgen naar om 8 uur*	yes, I listen to it at 8 o'clock every morning
*maar mijn man luistert **er** nooit naar*	but my husband never listens to it
de moeilijkheden in de economie?	the problems in the economy?
***daar** praat ik liever niet over*	I don't like to talk about them
*maar mijn vrouw praat **er** heel graag over*	but my wife likes to talk about them a lot

direct object:

het televisiejournaal?	the news on TV?
*nee, **dat** heb ik gisteravond niet gezien*	no, I didn't see it last night
*maar mijn man heeft **het** wel gezien*	but my husband did see it
de radionieuwsdienst van 8 uur?	the 8 o'clock news on the radio?
*nee, **die** heb ik niet gehoord*	no, I didn't hear it
*maar mijn vrouw heeft **hem** wel gehoord*	but my wife did hear it
de moeilijkheden in de economie?	the problems in the economy?
***die** vind ik niet zo groot*	I don't think they're too great
maar mijn vrouw wel	but my wife does
*die vindt **ze** heel erg groot*	she thinks they're very great

Summary

In general, the first time one uses a pronoun one would use *daar* + preposition and the second, third etc. time *er* + preposition. However this is not a fixed rule. One is not obliged to use *daar* the first time. *Er* is also correct. See lesson 14, E. 2–5, 9, 14.

The same holds for *die/dat* versus *hem/het/ze*. It is perfectly all right to use *hem/het/ze* the first time. See lesson 9, E. 6–10.

2.1.3 Word order

Pay attention to the fact that *daar/er/waar* and preposition are often split up:

waarover *hebt u gisteren gepraat?*	
waar *hebt u gisteren* **over** *gepraat?*	what did you talk about yesterday?
waarover *gaat u vandaag praten?*	
waar *gaat u vandaag* **over** *praten?*	what are you going to talk about today?
waarover *praat u vandaag?*	
waar *praat u vandaag* **over?**	what are you talking about today?
daarover *praten wij nooit*	
daar *praten wij nooit* **over**	that's something we never talk about
daarover *hebben wij nog nooit gepraat*	
daar *hebben wij nog nooit* **over** *gepraat*	that's something we've never talked about
daarover *willen ze liever niet praten*	
daar *willen ze liever niet* **over** *praten*	that's something they prefer not to talk about
wij hebben **er** *nog nooit* **over** *gepraat*	we've never talked about it
wij praten **er** *nooit* **over**	we never talk about it
wij willen **er** *nooit* **over** *praten*	we don't ever want to talk about it

2.1.4 *Met, naartoe, vandaan*

There are three prepositions which change their form if they occur with *waar, daar, hier* or *er*.

1. *Met* becomes *mee* (E. 5):

Anneke speelt vaak met haar pop,	Anneke often plays with her puppet
maar Jan speelt er ook wel eens **mee**	but Jan sometimes plays with it too
waar spelen ze **mee?**	what do they play with?

2. *Naar* becomes *naartoe* when the verb expresses movement. In other cases it remains unchanged (E. 3):

ik ga naar de film	I'm going to the cinema
ga jij er ook **naartoe?**	are you going too?
we gaan er **naartoe**	we're going

Kees luistert naar de radio,	Kees listens to the radio,
*maar ik luister er niet **naar***	but I don't listen to it
*waar luistert hij **naar?***	what does he listen to?

3. *Van* becomes *vandaan* when the verb expresses movement. In other cases it remains *van:*

hij komt net van Utrecht	he's just arrived from Utrecht
*kom jij daar ook **vandaan?***	is that where you've just come from too?
*waar kom jij **vandaan?***	where have you come from?
Kees houdt van pannekoeken	Kees likes pancakes
*houd jij daar ook **van?***	do you like them too?
*waar houd jij **van?***	what do you like?

N.B. *hij komt uit Engeland*   he comes from England
      kom jij daar ook vandaan?   do you come from there too?

2.2 WORD ORDER IN SUBCLAUSES

In the dialogue of this lesson a number of clauses occur which begin with *als:*

*als ze 's morgens **opstaan*** (1.24)	when they get up in the morning
*als ze een brief **krijgen*** (1.25)	when they get a letter
*als ze een aardig meisje **ontmoeten*** (1.26)	when they meet a nice girl
*als ze **doodgaan*** (1.27)	when they die
ze blijven maar zingen! (1.28)	they keep on singing

These are examples of subclauses. It is important to note that in a subclause the PV is always at the end. The PVs in the above examples are in bold face.

If the subclause comes before the main clause, the PV of the main clause immediately follows the subclause. The complete subclause comprises the first constituent of the sentence (see E.15).

als ze opstaan, zingen ze	when they get up they sing
's morgens zingen ze	in the morning they sing
ze zingen als ze opstaan	they sing when they get up
ze zingen 's morgens	they sing in the morning

There is more information about the place of the PV in main clauses and in subclauses in appendix C1.

3 FURTHER REMARKS

3.1 *MAAR*

Maar has many meanings. It mostly occurs in meanings 1 and 2 below.

1. Contrast, objection (in English: 'but')

Els heeft TV gekeken	Els has been watching TV
maar ik heb de krant gelezen	but I have been reading the paper
maar ik hoor niets (1.51)	but I can't hear anything
de volgende keer kijken we niet alleen,	the next time we won't only watch
maar dan luisteren we ook (1.70–71)	but we'll listen as well
Kees nodigt Anneke uit voor een opera	Kees invites Anneke to the opera
maar Anneke houdt helemaal niet van opera	but Anneke doesn't like opera at all

2. Restriction (often in combination with *alleen*) (in English: 'only')

ik heb maar twee gulden bij me	I have only two guilders on me
ik heb maar weinig Nederlanders ontmoet	I've only met a few Dutch people
Marie-Louise is maar 19 jaar	Marie-Louise is only 19
ik spreek geen Nederlands,	I don't speak Dutch,
ik spreek alleen maar Engels	I only speak English
ik ga alleen maar even sigaretten halen,	I'm only going to get some cigarettes,
ik ben meteen weer terug	I'll be back straightaway
hij kan er alleen maar om lachen (1.33)	all he can do is laugh at it

Of the other meanings of *maar* two instances occur in this lesson:

3. In sentences that express advice or a suggestion to do something *maar* means 'just go ahead', 'I don't mind' etc.

doe het maar	go ahead and do it
ga maar even mee	why don't you just come along?
zet maar rustig aan hoor (1.49)	just switch it on, don't worry about me
geef maar hier	give it here
toe maar	come on, do it
kom maar	come on

4. Continuity of an action or event or continually staying away from an event

ze blijven maar zingen (1.28)	they just go on singing
hij komt maar niet!	he still hasn't come (shows exasperation)
op vergaderingen praten ze maar	at meetings they just talk
en praten ze maar	and talk

LESSON 14

3.2 MISCELLANEOUS REMARKS

(1.4) *ik houd helemaal niet van opera's*   I don't like operas at all

(1.5) *ik heb naar die reportage gekeken*   I watched the (sports) report on the
           op het tweede net   2nd channel

The two Dutch TV channels are called *Nederland I* and *Nederland II*. The Dutch often refer to them as *'t eerste net* and *'t tweede net* ('the first channel' and 'the second channel'), or simply *één* and *twee*, e.g.

wat komt er vanavond op twee?   what's on 2 tonight?

The four national radio broadcasting stations are called *Hilversum I, II, III*, and *IV*. (See also the supplementary glossary on page 123 of the course book).

(1.9) *al dat geraas*   all that noise

(1.10) *daar houd ik nu helemaal niet van*   now that's something I don't like at all

Nou (sometimes spelt *nu*) reinforces the contrast.

Kees houdt van motorraces,   Kees likes motor racing,
daar houdt Anneke helemaal niet van   but Anneke doesn't like it at all

(1.12) *waar hebben jullie het over?*   what are you talking about?

het hebben over = *praten over*   to talk about

(1.17) *ja, dat wil zeggen*   yes, that is to say

Dat wil zeggen is usually shortened to *d.w.z.* and means 'that is to say', 'i.e.'.

(1.23) *de hele tijd*   all the time

(1.24) *als ze 's morgens opstaan*   when they get up in the morning

Als occurs in this lesson in two functions:

1. as a conjunction of time

als ze doodgaan (1.27)   when they die

2. as a conjunction of comparison

hij is net als jij (1.32)   he's just like you

(1.38) *spelen met vuur*   to play with fire (literally and figuratively)

(1.46) *Jaap en ik houden erg van*   Jaap and I like organ music very much
           orgelmuziek

Erg has several meanings:

1. 'very much' (1.46)

2. 'very'

zo'n orgelconcert is erg leuk (1.67)   organ concerts are very nice

(1.53) *het toestel wordt oud*   the set's getting old

oud worden   to get old

(1.54) *soms valt het geluid weg*   sometimes the noise goes off

wegvallen   to fall off, to disappear

(1.57) *dat staat tenminste in de gids*   at least that's what it says in the radio and
                                         TV guide

Gids usually means 'guide', but in this case it is short for *omroepgids, radiobode* (a weekly magazine announcing radio and television programmes).

LESSON 15

1 SUMMARY OF THE DIALOGUE

Anneke prepares for her evening out; she's looking for her black purse. Her sister knows where it is because she has 'borrowed' it. Anneke can't find her handkerchief and her key either. While they are looking for it, Niek arrives. He wants to borrow a bike.

Pay attention to expessions like: *die/dat van mij/jou* etc.

2 GRAMMAR

2.1 POSSESSIVE CONSTRUCTIONS
2.1.1 Pronominal possessive constructions   E. 1, 2, 6, 7

Instead of *mijn boek* you can also say *dat van mij* ('mine') or *het mijne* ('mine').
Here is a list of options:

mijn boek	*dat van mij*	*het mijne*
mijn jas	*die van mij*	*de mijne*
jouw boek	*dat van jou*	*het jouwe*
jouw jas	*die van jou*	*de jouwe*
uw boek	*dat van u*	*het uwe*
uw jas	*die van u*	*de uwe*
zijn boek	*dat van hem*	*het zijne*
zijn jas	*die van hem*	*de zijne*
haar boek	*dat van haar*	*het hare*
haar jas	*die van haar*	*de hare*
ons boek	*dat van ons*	*het onze*
onze jas	*die van ons*	*de onze*
jullie boek	*dat van jullie*	–
jullie jas	*die van jullie*	–
hun boek	*dat van hun*	*het hunne*
hun jas	*die van hun*	*de hunne*
mijn boeken en jassen	*die van mij*	*de mijne*
jouw boeken en jassen	*die van jou*	*de jouwe*
uw boeken en jassen	*die van u*	*de uwe*
zijn boeken en jassen	*die van hem*	*de zijne*
haar boeken en jassen	*die van haar*	*de hare*
onze boeken en jassen	*die van ons*	*de onze*
jullie boeken en jassen	*die van jullie*	–
hun boeken en jassen	*die van hun*	*de hunne*

LESSON 15

E. 4, 5

2.1.2 Possessive constructions with a proper noun
van + name:

de fiets van Niek en het tasje van Anneke   Niek's bike and Anneke's handbag

name + *s:*

Nieks fiets en Anneke's tas   Niek's bike and Anneke's handbag
Kees' tas en Meta's foto   Kees' bag and Meta's photo

name + *z'n/dr* without stress:

Niek z'n fiets en Anneke d'r tasje
Kees z'n tas en Meta d'r foto

2.2 *ZETTEN, LEGGEN, STOPPEN, STAAN, LIGGEN, ZITTEN*

These verbs are used to indicate the position in which an object is placed (*zetten, leggen, stoppen*), or to indicate the position the object takes up (*staan, liggen, zitten*). Note that the first three verbs are transitive, while the second set are intransitive.

Below are a few rules for how these verbs are used to indicate the position(ing) of (concrete) objects.

1. When an object (i) is situated or (ii) is placed in a relatively closed space such as a cupboard, bag, suitcase, pocket or purse then in the case of (i) you use *zítten (in)* and in the case of (ii) the verbs *stoppen (in)* or *doen (in)*, e.g.

ik stop de portemonnee altijd in mijn tas   I always put the purse in my bag
                    (line 39)
maar nu zit hij er niet in (1.40)   but it's not there now
ik stop/doe het geld in mijn portemonnee   I put the money in my purse
het geld zit in mijn portemonnee   the money is in my purse

Generally speaking, *zitten* can here be seen as the result of *stoppen, doen.*

2. Most concrete objects may take up more than one position: a normal one and a less normal one. Think, for instance, of cups, plates, shoes, ash trays, chairs, cupboards, tables, trees, cars and bicycles, to name just a few. In Dutch you use:

zetten for the placing of an object in its normal position
leggen for the placing of an object in a position other than its normal one
staan when the object is in its normal position
liggen when the object is in a position other than its normal one

Here are some examples:

de fiets staat tegen de boom	the bike is standing against the tree
de fiets ligt onder de boom	the bike is lying under the tree
het bord staat op tafel	the plate is on the table
het bord ligt op de grond	the plate is on the floor

Sometimes more than one position may be considered normal, for instances with books, records, bags and cases. In such cases *staan* and *zetten* are used when the position is a vertical one and *liggen* and *leggen* when the position is horizontal, e.g.

ik zet het boek in de kast	(vertical)	I put the book on the shelf
het boek staat in de boekenkast	(vertical)	the book is on the shelf
ik leg het boek op tafel	(horizontal)	I put the book on the table
het boek ligt op tafel	(horizontal)	the book is on the table

If an object can only take up one position and no more, you use *liggen* and *leggen,* e.g. with keys, forks, knives, balls, apples, bananas etc. Here are some examples:

misschien ligt de sleutel op de grond	maybe the key is on the floor
of op de stoel (1.44)	or on the chair
hier ligt je sleutel, tussen je boeken (1.68)	here's your key, between your books
zal ik je sleutel op je bed leggen? (1.70)	shall I put your key on your bed?
het zakdoekje ligt in de kast	the handkerchief is in the cupboard

N.B. Of course, these objects can be put in a closed space, in which case the rules under 1. apply:

de sleutel zit in het slot	the key is in the lock
ik doe/stop de sleutel in het slot	I put the key in the lock

2.2.1 The conjugation of *zitten, zetten, leggen* and *liggen*

Careful attention should be paid to the conjugation of these two pairs of verbs. Many of the forms are similar.

ik	*zit*	*ik*	*zet*	*ik*	*leg*	*ik*	*lig*
je	*zit*	*je*	*zet*	*je*	*legt*	*je*	*ligt*
u	*zit*	*u*	*zet*	*u*	*legt*	*u*	*ligt*
hij	*zit*	*hij*	*zet*	*hij*	*legt*	*hij*	*ligt*
ze	*zit*	*ze*	*zet*	*ze*	*legt*	*ze*	*ligt*
het	*zit*	*het*	*zet*	*het*	*legt*	*het*	*ligt*
we	*zitten*	*we*	*zetten*	*we*	*leggen*	*we*	*liggen*
jullie	*zitten*	*jullie*	*zetten*	*jullie*	*leggen*	*jullie*	*liggen*
ze	*zitten*	*ze*	*zetten*	*ze*	*leggen*	*ze*	*liggen*
ik heb gezeten		*ik heb gezet*		*ik heb gelegd*		*ik heb gelegen*	

91

LESSON 15

2.3 *DIE* AND *DAT*   E.8

In lesson 8, section 2.1.4 we saw that *die* and *dat* may replace a personal pronoun:

waar zit Els?	where's Els?
die zit in de tuin	she's sitting in the garden
zie je het huis?	can you see the house?
ja, dat zie ik	yes, I can
ja, dat staat in mijn kast (1.10)	yes, it's on my shelf

Dat may also refer to something in the previous sentence, or to the previous sentence as a whole.

zit Els in de tuin?	Is Els sitting in the garden?
ik weet het niet	
dat weet ik niet	I don't know
leent Marianne vaak iets van Anneke?	does Marianne often borrow something from Anneke?
ik denk het wel	
dat denk ik wel	I think so
hoe weet jij dat nou? (1.26)	how do you know?
nee, dat hoeft niet (1.31)	no, that won't be necessary

(See also lesson 14, section 2.1.2 and appendix D1.)

3 FURTHER REMARKS

3.1 *NOG*

1. Stressed *nog* means 'another', 'more':

wilt u nog een kopje koffie?	would you like another cup of coffee?
wacht even, er is nog iets	hold on, there's something else
kun je dat nog eens zeggen?	could you say that again?

2. Unstressed *nog* indicates that a certain number of things or beings are not yet at an end and that there is still something left, or that a certain period of time is not yet over:

ik héb er nog wel een (1.32)	I still have one
heb jij nog een paar kwártjes voor me?	have you got a few 'kwartjes' left?
zijn er nog éieren in huis?	are there any eggs left in the house?
hoevéél nog?	how many more?
hoevér nog?	how much further?

wacht even, er is nog iets	hold on, there's something left
dat was nog geen tién minuten geleden	that wasn't ten minutes ago (= less than)
wat wil je nog méér?	what more do you want?
en nu ben ik mijn húissleutel ook nog kwijt (1.33)	and now I've lost my front door key too
heb je hem vandáág nog gebruikt? (1.37)	have you used it today?
ja, vanmórgen nog (1.38)	yes, this morning
wilt u nog kóffie voor u weggaat?	do you want more coffee before you leave?
ik ben nog niet kláár	I'm not finished yet
wácht nog even alsjeblieft	wait a minute please
ik ben nog nooit naar het museum Boymans geweest	I've never been to the Boymans museum

N.B. *tot nóg toe = tot nú toe*

3.2 MISCELLANEOUS REMARKS

(1.15) *je hebt **toch zelf** een tasje?*	you've got a bag of your own, haven't you?
(1.16) *waarom pak je dat van mij **dan?***	then why do you take mine?
(1.24) *dat is **in de was***	it's in the laundry
(1.29) *jij leent ook **maar** alles!*	you're always borrowing!
(1.35) *zo is het al **erg** genoeg*	it's bad enough as it is
(1.41) *hij zit **vast** in je jaszak*	it's more than likely in your coat pocket
see lesson 9, section 3 (1.29)	
(1.54) *daar heb je niets mee te maken*	that's none of your business
iets te maken hebben met	to have something to do with
(1.67) *ze is hem kwijt*	she's lost it
iets kwijt zijn	to have lost something

LESSON 16

1 SUMMARY OF THE DIALOGUE

Kees is looking for new digs because he has to leave the room he has now. He has already been given several addresses, but he hasn't succeeded yet. He and John go to the Twentestraat by bike to inspect a room. When they get there, somebody else has already rented it.

Pay attention to the construction: PV*zijn* + *aan* + *het* + infinitive

e.g. *wat ben je aan het doen?* (1.1.)
  ik ben de krant aan het lezen (1.3)

2 GRAMMAR

2.1 THE CONSTRUCTION PV*ZIJN* + *AAN* + *HET* + INFINITIVE   E. 1–5

This construction is used to indicate that a certain action is in progress. For this, English uses the continuative (progressive form, –ing form).

ik ben aan het eten	I am eating
hij is aan het fietsen	he is cycling
zij zijn aan het voetballen	they are playing football
hallo Kees, wat ben je aan het doen? (line 1)	hello Kees, what are you doing?
ik ben de krant aan het lezen (1.3)	I am reading the paper

Objects and adjuncts follow the PV and precede *aan* + *het* + infinitive

ik ben een kamer aan het zoeken	I'm looking for a room
ik ben allang aan het zoeken	I've been looking for quite a while

This construction occurs only with verbs denoting an activity, but not with motion and other verbs:

hij ligt op de bank	he is lying on the couch
het schilderij hangt aan de muur	the painting is hanging on the wall
hij komt	he's coming
hij gaat naar de bakker	he's going to the baker's

2.2 VERBS DENOTING A MODE OF TRANSPORT

E. 6–8

Verbs which denote some mode of transport and which do not take an object, such as

fietsen	to cycle
lopen	to walk
rijden	to drive, to ride
vliegen	to fly
varen	to sail, to go by boat

sometimes have *zijn* and sometimes have *hebben* as auxiliaries in the perfect.

Zijn is used when the direction and goal of the movement are mentioned:

ik ben naar Amsterdam gereden	I drove to Amsterdam
ik ben er naartoe gereden	I drove there
we zijn naar de Twentestraat gefietst	we cycled to the Twentestraat
daar ben ik naartoe gefietst (1.32)	I cycled there

In all other cases we use **hebben:**

ik heb de hele dag gelopen	I've been walking all day
we hebben in de stad gefietst	we've been cycling in town
ik heb de hele morgen gefietst (1.22)	I've been cycling all morning

3   FURTHER REMARKS

3.1 *TOCH*

Note the following examples of *toch:*

dat zié je toch! (1.12)	you can see that, can't you?!
dat heb ik toch gézegd!	I said so, didn't I?!
ze hebben toch ópgebeld!	they phoned, didn't they?!

See also lesson 5, section 3.4; lesson 10, section 3.4; and lesson 12, section 3 (1.54).

3.2 MISCELLANEOUS REMARKS

(1.7) *moet je van je kamer af?*	do you have to give up your room?
(1.17) *maar nee hoor . . .*	but nothing doing . . .
(1.24) *maar het was allemaal niets*	but it was no good
(1.37) *een paar keer*	a number of times
(1.38) *maar steeds geen gehoor*	but there was never any answer
(1.42) *ik fiets **met je mee***	I'll go **with you** (by bike)

(1.47-48) *meneer,* **kunt u ons ook zeggen** can you tell us the way to
               waar de Twentestraat is?   the Twentestraat?
      This is a polite phrase used when asking for information.
      N.B. The last part of the sentence is a subclause. The PV therefore comes at the end.
      (E. 15)

(1.70)	*mevrouw, u hebt een kamer te huur,*	(Madam) you have a room to let,
	heb ik gehoord	I've heard
	te huur	to let
	te koop	for sale
	ik heb een huis te koop	I have a house for sale
	het huis is te koop	the house is for sale

(1.71) *dat*
       het *spijt me*   I'm sorry

LESSON 17

1 SUMMARY OF THE DIALOGUE

John has bought a second-hand car. He takes Kees for a drive. First they go to a petrol station, because there is hardly any petrol left. On the way they run into someone with tyre trouble. It's a girl. John changes her tyre. After a while the man from the road service turns up, but they don't need him anymore.

Pay attention to sentences with *want* and *omdat*.

2 GRAMMAR

2.1 *OMDAT* AND *WANT*   E. 4, 5, 14
2.1.1 Subclauses beginning with *omdat*

In this type of sentence the PV takes the last, or last but one, place.
See also lesson 14, section 2.2 and appendix C1.

*ik mag niet naar buiten omdat ik ziek **ben***	I can't go out because I'm ill
*ik mag niet naar buiten omdat ik ziek geweest **ben***	I can't go out because I have been ill
*ja, en omdat hij zijn brommer verkocht **heeft,** is hij er niet*	yes, and because he's sold his moped, he's not there
*ik kan niet naar de film, omdat ik **moet** werken*	I can't go to the cinema because I have to work
*ik moet nu nog naar de kruidenier, omdat ik geen thee meer **heb*** (line 3-4)	now I only have to go to the grocer's, because I'm out of tea
*omdat daar alle prijzen inclusief **zijn*** (1.40)	because all the prices include service

2.1.2 *Want*

Clauses beginning with *want* have normal word order. *Want* never answers the question 'why?'.
A clause with *want* never occurs independently and cannot precede the main clause.

ik moet even tanken, want mijn benzine is op (1.27–28)	I must have some petrol, because I haven't got any left
waarom blijf je thuis?	why are you staying in?
omdat ik ziek ben	because I'm ill
omdat ik ziek ben blijf ik thuis	because I'm ill I'm staying in
ik blijf thuis omdat ik ziek ben	I'm staying in because I'm ill
blijf je thuis?	are you staying in?
ja, ik blijf thuis want ik ben ziek	yes, I'm staying in, because I'm ill

LESSON 17

3   FURTHER REMARKS

3.1 *WEL*

dat zal wel gaan (1.36)   I think that'll be possible

As was noted in lessons 6 and 10, unstressed *wel* can express the speaker's willingness to do something. But it can also express an assumption on the part of the speaker that something is or is not the case. In this case *wel* often goes together with the auxiliary verb *zullen*, as is the case in 1.36. Here are some further examples:

jullie zullen wel móé zijn   I suppose you'll be tired
jullie zullen wel niét moe zijn   I suppose you won't be tired
hij zal wel vróég thuis komen   I presume he's coming home early
hij zal wel niét vroeg thuis komen   I presume he's not coming home early
u zult wel hónger hebben   I suppose you'll be hungry
u zult wel géén honger hebben   I suppose you won't be hungry

3.2 *ZEKER*

Zeker, stressed as well as unstressed, has many meanings. Stressed, it means 'definitely', 'sure', 'certainly'. See also Lesson 10, section 3.2.

dan moeten we zéker stoppen (1.45)   then we must definitely stop
ik kom zéker   I'm definitely coming
het is zéker 20 minuten fietsen   it must be 20 minutes on the bike
     van mijn huis naar het station   from my house to the station
ik weet zéker dat John ziek is   I know for sure that John is ill
ik weet het niet zéker   I'm not sure
zéker!   of course
jazéker!   (yes) of course

3.3 MISCELLANEOUS REMARKS

(1.4) *omdat ik geen thee meer heb*   because I'm out of tea
    geen + noun + *meer hebben*   to have no more of something
    (E. 2)
(1.10) *ik ben hier al uren mijn auto*   I've been cleaning my car here **for hours**
    aan het schoonmaken
(1.11) *en jij merkt het niet eens*   and you don't even notice
(1.72) *en naar mij heeft ze niet eens gekeken*   and she never even looked at me
(1.23) *zullen we een eindje gaan rijden?*   shall we go for a drive?
    een eindje   a short distance
    Note also:
    ik ga een eindje fietsen   I'm going for a ride on the bike
    ik ga een eindje lopen   I'm going for a walk

	we moeten nog maar een klein eindje, en dan zijn we er	we've only a little way still to go, and then we'll be there
(1.24)	*het dak maak ik een andere keer wel schoon*	I'll wash the roof some other time
	een andere keer	another time; some other time
(1.30)	*maakt u hem maar vol*	fill her up, please
(1.34)	*maakt u er maar 25 gulden van*	make it 25 guilders
(1.37)	*móét je hier eigenlijk een fooi geven?*	do you have to give a tip here?
(1.51)	*en er komt maar geen wegenwacht*	and the man from the road service just won't come
(1.57)	*een lekke band*	a flat tyre
(1.61)	*dan ga ik weer verder*	then I'll be off
(1.65)	*heel hartelijk dank*	thank you very, very much
(1.69)	*ja, dat heb ik gemerkt!*	yes, I noticed
(1.70)	*aan één stuk door*	all the time; continuously

LESSON 18

1 SUMMARY OF THE DIALOGUE

Kees calls Mrs Verhage because she has a room to let. That afternoon he inspects the room, and Mrs Verhage gives him some information. He decides to take the room.

Pay attention to the relative pronoun, e.g. *de kamer die u te huur hebt* . . .

2 GRAMMAR

2.1 RELATIVE PRONOUNS   E. 1–4, 17

The demonstrative pronouns *die/dat* are used as relative pronouns.

Die refers to – a singular *de*-word
                     – all plural nouns
                     – all people
Dat refers to – a *het*-word

Their forms in object function are identical with the subject forms.

singular:	*de man die* (subject) *daar loopt is mijn vriend*	the man walking over there is my friend
	de man die (object) *u daar ziet is mijn vriend*	the man that you see over there is my friend
plural:	*de mannen die* (subject) *daar lopen zijn mijn vrienden*	the men walking over there are my friends
	de mannen die (object) *u daar ziet zijn mijn vrienden*	the men that you see over there are my friends
singular:	*hier is de kamer die* (subject) *pas geverfd is*	here is the room which has just been painted
	hier is de kamer die (subject) *ik voor u heb*	here is the room which I have for you
plural:	*hier zijn de kamers die* (subject) *pas geverfd zijn*	here are the rooms which have just been painted
	hier zijn de kamers die (object) *ik voor u heb*	here are the rooms which I have for you
singular:	*het bureau dat* (object) *ik heb kan ik toch meenemen?* (line 60)	I can bring the desk I've got now, can't I?
	het bureau dat (subject) *voor het raam staat is van mij*	the desk which is in front of the window is mine

plural: *de bureaus die* (object) *we hebben*   the desks which we have are very expensive
  zijn erg duur
  de bureaus die (subject) *voor*   the desks which are in front of the window
  het raam staan zijn erg duur   are very expensive

N.B. A relative pronoun introduces a clause which is an adjunct to a noun or pronoun, (a relative clause). The word order in a relative clause is the same as in the subordinate clause (see lesson 14, section 2.2, as well as appendix C1).

2.2 SENTENCES WITH MORE THAN ONE AUXILIARY   E. 16

In exercise 16 we see sentences with more than one auxiliary. The following rules apply to their form and position in the sentence:

1. If there is one auxiliary in the sentence, it takes the place and the form of the PV. The main verb becomes an infinitive and is removed to the last position in the sentence (not in the perfect tense).

ik bekijk de kamer   I inspect the room
ik kom de kamer bekijken   I've come to inspect the room

2. If a second auxiliary is added, this takes the form and the place of the PV. The first auxiliary then becomes an infinitive and precedes the infinitive of the main verb.

ik kom de kamer bekijken
ik zal de kamer komen bekijken   I will come to inspect the room

ik betaal de huur   I pay the rent
ik kom de huur betalen   I've come to pay the rent
ik zal de huur komen betalen   I will come to pay the rent

3   FURTHER REMARKS

(1.10) *en nu is het een enorme rommel*   and now the room is in a terrible mess
  in de kamer
(1.18) *ik zal u even voorgaan*   I will lead the way
  This phrase is used if one shows a person the way by going before him. If, instead, one gives precedence to someone, one says:
  gaat uw gang or *ga je gang*   after you
(1.21) *op het zuiden*   facing South
(1.32) *maar wat mij betreft*   but as far as I am concerned

LESSON 18

(1.38) *en wat voor meubels komen er?*   and what will there be by way of furniture?
One way of enquiring after the characteristics of something is to use the phrase **wat voor** (+ indefinite article) + noun ('what sort of' + noun):

wat voor (een) boek zoek je?   what kind of book are you looking for?
wat voor (een) meubels komen er? what kind of furniture is there going to be?

(1.39) *zo*   in a minute; in a moment

(1.50) *kan ik een **eigen** bel aanleggen?*   can I put my own bell in?
Eigen ('own'; 'of my/your/etc. own') as an adjective is not inflected.
Kees heeft een eigen bel as against *Kees heeft een harde bel*
mijn eigen huis   *mijn oude huis*

(1.65) *vooruit betalen*   to pay in advance

(1.69) *eind april*   at the end of April

LESSON 19

1   SUMMARY OF THE DIALOGUE

John is shown around a newly built hospital. There is one ward which has not yet been put into use, so he can take a good look at everything – the patients' rooms, the ward kitchen and the so-called 'flower station'.

Pay attention to passive sentences, such as *de bedden worden laag gezet.*

2   GRAMMAR

2.1   PASSIVE SENTENCES   E. 4–7, 9, 10, 13, 16
2.1.1 In this lesson many passive sentences occur. These are sentences like:

*alleen tijdens de rust **wordt de radio***	the radio is only switched off by the nurse
door de zuster afgezet (line 34)	during the midday rest period

Passive sentences are related to active sentences in the following way:

1. The object of the active sentence becomes subject of the passive sentence.
2. The subject of the active sentence is optionally represented in the passive sentence by a phrase beginning with *door* ('by'), which indicates the performer(s) of the activity.
3. The verb of the active sentence becomes the past participle of the passive sentence.

The passive sentence is formed by means of the **auxiliary *worden.***

active	passive
de zuster wast de patiënt	*de patiënt wordt (door de zuster) gewassen*
subject PV object	subject auxiliary (performer) past participle

het ziekenhuis kiest het programma   *het programma wordt door het ziekenhuis gekozen*
de patiënt zet de radio aan   *de radio wordt door de patiënt aangezet*

present tense forms

ik	*word*	*gewassen (door de zuster)*	I am washed (by the nurse)
je	*wordt*	*gewassen (door de zuster)*	you are washed etc.
u	*wordt*	*gewassen (door de zuster)*	
hij	*wordt*	*gewassen (door de zuster)*	
ze	*wordt*	*gewassen (door de zuster)*	
het	*wordt*	*gewassen (door de zuster)*	
we	*worden*	*gewassen (door de zuster)*	
jullie	*worden*	*gewassen (door de zuster)*	
ze	*worden*	*gewassen (door de zuster)*	

LESSON 19

2.1.2 A passive sentence may be used when you do not know who it is that performs the action or when it does not really matter who it is, in which case the phrase with *door* is omitted.

een patiënt die ernstig ziek is,	a patient who is seriously ill
wordt alleen gelegd (1.46)	is given a room of his own

Often a corresponding active sentence would have *ze* as subject, as can be seen in the following examples:

passive	active
het eten wordt hier klaar gemaakt	*ze maken hier het eten klaar*
de patiënten worden om 7 uur gewassen	*ze wassen de patienten om 7 uur*
dan worden de bedden hooggezet	*dan zetten ze de bedden hoog*

2.1.3 If the object of the active sentence is indefinite, it corresponds to an indefinite subject in the passive sentence. Then *er* must be added (cf. lesson 10, section 2.2):

ze bellen een dokter	*er wordt een dokter gebeld*
ze brengen bloemen mee	*er worden bloemen meegebracht*
ze zetten koffie	*er wordt koffie gezet*
ze verzorgen veel patiënten	*er worden veel patiënten verzorgd*
N.B. *ze verzorgen **de** patiënten*	***de** patiënten worden verzorgd*

2.1.4 Some active sentences with an intransitive verb have a passive equivalent. The subject of these sentences is an indefinite pronoun. In the passive sentence *er* is added. Note that this type of passive sentence does not really have a standard equivalent in English. The meaning of a sentence like *er wordt niet hard gewerkt* is something like 'there's not any hard work being done'.

active	passive
ze zingen mooi	*er wordt mooi gezongen*
ze werken niet hard	*er wordt niet hard gewerkt*
ze lachen op de gang	*er wordt op de gang gelachen*
ze voetballen niet vaak	*er wordt niet vaak gevoetbald*

2.1.5 The passive of a sentence in the **perfect tense** is formed by means of the auxiliary ***zijn.*** The other formation rules are as described under 2.1.1.

de patiënt heeft de radio aangezet	*de radio is door de patiënt aangezet*
ze hebben de bedden hooggezet	*de bedden zijn hooggezet*
ze hebben de bloemen meegenomen	*er zijn bloemen meegenomen*
(see lesson 22, E. 9, 10)	

2.2 THE SUPERLATIVE
2.2.1 Form

The superlative is a form of the adjective. It is constructed by adding *-ste* to the undeclined form of the adjective:

groot – grootste	*het grootste boek*
klein – kleinste	*het kleinste meisje*
mooi – mooiste	*de mooiste huizen*
oud – oudste	*de oudste zoon*
dat is het gemakkelijkste (1.22)	that is the easiest solution
kijk, dat is de laagste stand	look, this is the lowest position
en dit is de hoogste (1.27–28)	and this is the highest

Some adjectives have an irregular superlative:

goed   – beste
weinig – minste
veel   – meeste
graag – liefste
N.B. *beste Kees* = dear Kees

2.2.2 The use of the superlative   E. 1–3

The superlative is used:
– to indicate the highest degree of the quality or characteristic expressed by the adjective
– if two things are compared

dit is het mooiste ziekenhuis van Nederland,	this is the most beautiful hospital in Holland,
zeggen ze (1.3)	they say
ik heb twee zoons: dit is de oudste	I have two sons: this is the elder
en dat is de jongste	and that is the younger
wil je het grootste of het kleinste stuk?	would you like to have the larger or the smaller part?

2.2.3 The predicative form of the superlative

The superlative used predicatively is formed as follows:

het + adjective + *st(e)*

Note that *het* here is neither an article nor a pronoun.

die tafel en dat kastje kosten veel,	the table and the cupboard cost a lot,
maar het bureau is toch wel het duurst(e)	but the desk is still the dearest

LESSON 19

Meta en Corrie zijn klein,　　　　　Meta and Corrie are small,
maar Wim is toch het kleinst(e)　　but Wim is the smallest

ik vind Corrie en Els wel aardig,　Corrie and Els are nice,
maar Anneke is het aardigst(e)　　but Anneke is the nicest, I think

3　FURTHER REMARKS

(1.5)	*in elk geval*	in any case, at any rate
(1.6)	*het ziekenhuis **is** nu bijna*	the hospital is now almost
	*helemaal **in gebruik***	totally operational
	in gebruik zijn　– gebruikt worden	to be in use
(1.8)	*in gebruik nemen – gaan gebruiken*	to put into use
(1.17)	*we hebben hier **hele** praktische*	we have very practical beds here
	bedden	

Hele in the sense of *zeer* is properly speaking an adverb but it is usually declined as an adjective: *hele praktische bedden*
　　　　but: *een heel aardig meisje*

(1.23)	*want dan **hoeven** de zusters*	because then the nurses
	niet te bukken	don't need to stoop

The usual negative of *moeten* is *niet hoeven* (+ *te* + infinitive)

moet ik naar huis gaan?	do I have to go home?
nee, dat hoeft niet	no, you don't have to
nee, je hoeft niet naar huis te gaan	no, you don't have to go home
moet ik de dokter nu roepen?	do I have to call the doctor now?
nee, je hoeft hem nu niet te roepen	no, you don't have to call him now
dat moet je niet doen	you mustn't do that
dat hoef je niet te doen	you needn't do that
(E. 12–15)	

(1.30)	*en dit apparaat heeft zeker*	and this device has something to do
	iets met de radio te maken?	with the radio, I presume?
	(n) iets te maken hebben met	have something (nothing) to do with
(1.41)	*zonder dat de patiënt een*	without the patient becoming a number
	nummer wordt	

Here *worden* means 'to become'. Note the difference in use between this *worden* and that in the passive sentence *de patiënt wordt verzorgd.*
　cf. *ze is vorige maand 19 geworden*　she became 19 last month
　　　　　　(lesson 12, 1.14)
　　het toestel wordt oud　　　　the set's getting old
　　　　　　(lesson 14, 1.53)

(1.54)	*die hebben het al druk genoeg*	they're busy enough as it is
(1.58)	*dat **spaart** een heleboel werk*	that **saves** a lot of work
(1.65)	*hier maken we melk warm **en zo***	here is where we warm milk and **things like that**

LESSON 20

1 SUMMARY OF THE DIALOGUE

Anneke notices that John has started wearing glasses, and asks him which optician he has consulted. It is Dr van Duin. She tells John a lot about Dr van Duin; she knows him because he is a friend of her father's.

In the dialogue of this lesson the simple past tense occurs rather often. Pay attention to the various forms and to the pronunciation of *hij* after a simple past tense. Listen carefully to the tape. E.g. /werktə-d-ie/
   /zei-d-ie/
   /was-t-ie/

2 GRAMMAR

2.1 THE SIMPLE PAST TENSE
2.1.1 Form

The simple past tense is a verb form indicating past time. The formation is not the same for all verbs. As in the case of the perfect tense (see lesson 10, section 2.1), the differences can be explained by the fact that all verbs are subdivided in three types: **weak, strong and irregular ones.**

2.1.1.1 Weak verbs   E. 1, 2

As you know, the past participle of weak verbs is formed as follows:

ge + verb stem + $\begin{matrix} d \\ t \end{matrix}$ *gewoond*
        gekookt

The verb stem is the basis for the formation of the simple past tense as well:

the singular form of the simple past tense is: stem + $\begin{matrix} de \\ te \end{matrix}$ *woonde*
        kookte

the plural   form of the simple past tense is: stem + $\begin{matrix} den \\ ten \end{matrix}$ *woonden*
        kookten

For the whole of the singular there is only one form. The same goes for the plural, with the exception of *u: u woonde.*

singular	1.	*ik*	*woonde*	*werkte*
	2.	*je*	*woonde*	*werkte*
		u	*woonde*	*werkte*
	3.	*hij*	*woonde*	*werkte*
		ze	*woonde*	*werkte*
		het	*woonde*	*werkte*
plural	1.	*we*	*woonden*	*werkten*
	2.	*jullie*	*woonden*	*werkten*
		u	*woonde*	*werkte*
	3.	*ze*	*woonden*	*werkten*

The rules for spelling and pronunciation as given in lessons 2, 3 and 10 are applicable here too.

2.1.1.2 Strong verbs

The simple past tense of strong verbs is formed as follows:
the vowel of the stem is changed; there is no suffix in the singular, and the plural takes *-en*.

infinitive	present tense	past tense singular	past tense plural
beginnen	*ik begin*	*ik begon*	*we begonnen*
lopen	*ik loop*	*ik liep*	*we liepen*
vinden	*ik vind*	*ik vond*	*we vonden*
rijden	*ik rijd*	*ik reed*	*we reden*

Sometimes the plural has a longer vowel than the singular, though the spelling is identical.

infinitive	past tense singular	past tense plural
nemen	*nam*	*namen*/naamən/
eten	*at*	*aten* /aatən/
geven	*gaf*	*gaven* /gaavən/

2.1.1.3 Irregular verbs   E.1–7

A number of verbs have an irregular simple past tense, e.g.

kunnen	*kon*	*konden*
zijn	*was*	*waren*
hebben	*had*	*hadden*
zeggen	*zei*	*zeiden*
houden	*hield*	*hielden*
kopen	*kocht*	*kochten*

For the strong and irregular verbs, see also the list in the course book (page 216) and appendix B2.

2.1.2 Using the simple past and the perfect

Explicit rules about when to use the simple past tense and when the perfect are hard to give. Here are some general guidelines.

The **simple past tense** is mostly used to tell what happened or how the situation was at a (implicitly or explicitly) given moment or period in the past.

waar was je gisteren om 4 uur?	where were you yesterday at 4 o'clock?
ik was bij de oogarts	I was at the optician's
wat deed Dr. van Duin na de bevrijding?	what did Dr van Duin do after the liberation?
hij ging met zijn vrouw naar Suriname	he went with his wife to Surinam

The simple past tense is often used in stories and for recounting things that occurred in the past.

The **perfect** is mostly used to indicate an act or situation which has ended; the main interest is in the present result of the past action or event.

ik heb lekker geslapen	I slept well (i.e. I'm not tired anymore)
heb je dat boek al gelezen?	have you read that book? (i.e. do you know it?)

In Dutch many sentences in the perfect have an adjunct of time:

*ik heb Kees **vorig jaar** op de boot ontmoet*	I met Kees on the boat last year
*waar ben je **gisteren** geweest?*	where were you yesterday?
*de trein is **5 minuten geleden** vertrokken*	the train left 5 minutes ago

2.2   THE PASSIVE   E. 10, 11

In E. 10 and 11 we see passive sentences in the simple past:

active	passive
*ze **ruimen** de keuken op*	*de keuken **wordt** opgeruimd*
*ze **ruimden** de keuken op*	*de keuken **werd** opgeruimd*
*ze **wassen** de patiënten*	*de patiënten **worden** gewassen*
*ze **wasten** de patiënten*	*de patiënten **werden** gewassen*

ik	*werd*	*gewassen*
je	*werd*	*gewassen*
u	*werd*	*gewassen*
hij	*werd*	*gewassen*
ze	*werd*	*gewassen*
het	*werd*	*gewassen*
we	*werden*	*gewassen*
jullie	*werden*	*gewassen*
ze	*werden*	*gewassen*

LESSON 20

3   FURTHER REMARKS

(1.3) *ik had de laatste tijd nogal*   I have been troubled with headaches lately
        last van hoofdpijn
        last hebben van   to be troubled with; to be bothered by
        *ik heb **geen** last van hoofdpijn*   I don't get troubled by headaches
        ik heb er geen last van   I don't get troubled by them

(1.13) *hij vertelt graag over vroeger*   he likes telling stories about the old days

(1.14) *o ja? Hij zei anders niet veel*   oh, does he? He didn't say very much really

(1.15) *als hij met een patiënt bezig is*   when he is busy with a patient
        bezig zijn met   to be busy with

(1.16) *maar hij heeft wel **het een en ander***   but he has gone through quite a lot
        meegemaakt

(1.21) *de jaren dertig*   the thirties

(1.22) *er waren toen veel mensen*   there were many people in those days
        die het moeilijk hadden   who suffered much hardship
        het moeilijk hebben   to have difficulties; to suffer hardship

(1.28) *en beurzen waren er haast niet*   and there were hardly any grants
        een beurs   a grant
        haast niet   almost not; hardly
        haast nooit (1.47)   hardly ever

(1.30) *ik dacht in Leiden*   in Leiden, I think

(1.34) *onder andere in een ziekenhuis*   including in a hospital
        onder andere (often o.a.)   among others/other things; including

(1.36) *hij deed **van alles***   he did all kinds of things

(1.45) *hoelang deed hij **wel niet***   how long did it take him to finish his
        over zijn studie?   studies then? It must have been quite a
                                                                                    long time

(1.49) *binnen negen jaar*   within nine years
        in minder dan negen jaar   in less than nine years

(1.54) *zodat hij genoeg verdiende*   so that he earned enough
        om rond te komen   to make ends meet
        Zodat is a conjunction introducing a subclause. Pay attention to the word order.
        (E. 6)

(1.56) *zijn studie duurde bij elkaar dus*   so his studies took 15 years in all
        15 jaar
        bij elkaar   all in all
        Often *bij elkaar* is pronounced /bij məkaar/

(1.57) *hij was 33 **toen** hij een*   he was 33 before he was able to start
        praktijk kon beginnen   a practice
        Toen here means 'when' (see also lesson 21, section 2.3.3).

(1.60) *tegen het einde van de oorlog*   towards the end of the war
        trouwde hij   he got married

(1.69) *zo nu en dan*   every now and then

LESSON 21

1   SUMMARY OF THE DIALOGUE

Els and Jaap have just moved house. Kees comes to see their new flat. Els shows him everything and talks about the advantages and disadvantages of the flat as compared with their former home.

Pay attention to the comparative: *mooier, lichter, nieuwer* etc.

2   GRAMMAR

2.1   THE COMPARATIVE

In this lesson many adjectives take the comparative form. The comparative is used to express the notion that a certain entity possesses more of a certain quality than another entity. The comparative, then, is always concerned with comparing two things.

alles is hier mooier en nieuwer en lichter   everything is more beautiful, newer
                              (line 15)   and lighter here

2.1.1 Form

The comparative is formed by adding *-er(e)* to the undeclined form of the adjective.

	comparative	superlative (see lesson 19)	
mooi	*mooier(e)*	*mooist(e)*	beautiful
klein	*kleiner(e)*	*kleinst(e)*	small
nieuw	*nieuwer(e)*	*nieuwst(e)*	new
licht	*lichter(e)*	*lichtst(e)*	light
leuk	*leuker(e)*	*leukst(e)*	nice
schoon	*schoner(e)*	*schoonst(e)*	clean
groot	*groter(e)*	*grootst(e)*	big, larger
breed	*breder(e)*	*breedst(e)*	wide, broad
smal	*smaller(e)*	*smalst(e)*	narrow

If the adjective ends in *-r*, the comparative is formed by adding *-der(e)*:

duur	*duurder(e)*	*duurst(e)*	expensive
ver	*verder(e)*	*verst(e)*	far
helder	*helderder(e)*	*helderst(e)*	bright
zwaar	*zwaarder(e)*	*zwaarst(e)*	heavy

LESSON 21

Some adjectives (or adverbs) have an irregular comparative:

goed	beter(e)	best(e)
weinig	minder(e)	minst(e)
veel	meer	meest(e)
graag	liever	liefst(e)

2.1.2 The comparative is a special form of the adjective, and, consequently,   E. 1, 2, 6, 16
has the same characteristics as an adjective.

For the **attributively** used comparative, the same rules concerning the -e ending apply as
for the attributively used adjective (see lesson 11, section 2.1).

		het-words	**de**-words
singular	definite	het mooiere huis	de mooiere tafel
	indefinite	een mooier huis	een mooiere tafel
plural	definite	de mooiere huizen	de mooiere tafels
	indefinite	mooiere huizen	mooiere tafels

The comparative in **predicative** use always takes the short form (without -e).

dit ziekenhuis is modern,	this hospital is modern,
maar dat is nog moderner	but that one is more modern
dit boek is wel duur,	this book is expensive,
maar dat is nog duurder	but that one is more expensive

N.B. If we compare two individual entities we use the superlative:

Corrie is de oudste (1.47)	Corrie is the eldest
daarom heeft zij de grootste kamer	that's why she has the biggest room
(1.48)	

2.1.3 *Dan*   E. 3, 6, 7

The object/person/situation with which one compares something is not always mentioned,
e.g.

deze is wel langer maar niet zo breed (1.40)   this one is longer but not as wide

If the referent is mentioned, it is preceded by **dan** (although in spoken Dutch one often hears
als these days).

Corrie is ouder dan Wim	Corrie is older than Wim
ik vind hem aardiger dan jou (object)	I like him better than you
hij is aardiger dan jij (subject)	he is nicer than you are
die van Corrie is iets groter	Corrie's is slightly bigger than Wim's
dan die van Wim (1.46)	

112

Often the subject of comparison is described in a subclause. This subclause, then, is also introduced by *dan*:

we konden hier een dag eerder in	we could move in a day earlier
dan we dachten (1.11)	than we thought
hij is langer gebleven dan hij van plan was	he stayed longer than he had intended
hij is aardiger dan ik had gedacht	he is nicer than I had thought

2.1.4 A number of comparatives have additional meanings:

liever: 1. 'nicer', 'sweeter'
      2. 'more precisely', 'rather'

*ik vind Wim wel lief maar Corrie nog **liever***	I think Wim is nice but Corrie is nicer
*ik drink **graag** koffie,*	I like coffee,
*maar bij het ontbijt drink ik **liever** thee*	but for breakfast I prefer tea
*kijk, dit is de badkamer; of **liever**:*	look, this is the bathroom; or rather,
de douchecel, want we hebben geen bad	the shower, because we haven't got a bath

vroeger: 1. 'earlier than' (= *eerder*)
       2. 'before', 'in the past'

*kan je niet een beetje **vroeger***	can't you come a bit earlier
komen dan acht uur?	then eight o'clock
***vroeger** hadden we geen plaats voor*	we didn't have space for a fridge before,
een koelkast, maar nu in ons nieuwe huis wel	but in our new house we do
***vroeger** kon je alleen met de boot naar*	you used to be able to go to England
Engeland, maar nu kan je ook met het vliegtuig	by boat only, but now you can go by plane too

verder: 1. 'farther'
      2. 'further', 'additionally', 'else'

*Parijs is **verder** van Den Haag dan Brussel*	Paris is further from The Hague than Brussels
ik heb een jas en eèn nieuwe broek	I've bought a jacket and a new pair of
*gekocht en **verder** nog een paar sokken*	trousers and also a pair of socks
*en wat heb je **verder** nog gekocht?*	and what else have you bought?
*wilt u **verder** nog iets?*	would you like anything else?
*ga maar **verder** met lezen,*	go on reading,
ik wil je niet storen	I don't want to disturb you

eerder: 1. 'earlier than' (= *vroeger*)
      2. 'rather'

kan je niet een beetje **eerder** *komen dan 8 uur?*	can't you come a bit earlier than 8 o'clock?
we konden hier een dag **eerder** *in dan we dachten* (1.11)	we could move in a day earlier than we thought
ik ben niet echt ziek, ik ben **eerder** *moe*	I'm not really ill; rather I'm tired

later: 1. 'later than'
      2. 'afterwards', 'later on'

kan je niet een beetje **later** *komen dan 8 uur?*	can't you come a bit later than 8 o'clock?
eerst ontmoette Kees John King op de receptie	first Kees met John King at the reception
en **later** *zag hij ook Anneke van Kampen*	and later he also saw Anneke van Kampen
ik heb nu geen tijd voor je, maar **later** *vandaag misschien wel*	at the moment I have no time for you, but perhaps I will have later today

2.2 COMPARISON WITHOUT COMPARATIVE   E. 5, 7

If two compared entities possess a certain quality to the same degree, we use the following constructions to express this equivalence:

1. *net* + *zo* + adjective + *als*

deze kamer is **net zo** *groot* **als** *de vorige* (1.17)	this room is **just as** large **as** the one in your old house

2. *even* + adjective + *als*

Corrie is **even** *aardig* **als** *Wim*	Corrie is **as** nice **as** Wim
hij is **even** *lang gebleven* **als** *hij gedacht had* (E. 4)	he stayed **as** long **as** he had thought

3. *even* + adjective

de kamers zijn **even** *groot*	the rooms are **all the same size**
Piet en Jan zijn **even** *aardig*	Piet en Jan are **equally nice**
Piet en Jan zijn **even** *lang* *gebleven*	Piet and Jan stayed **for the same length of time**

A construction which, like the comparative, expresses the notion that two entities possess a certain quality in different degrees is:

niet + *zo* + adjective + *als*

*deze kamer is **niet zo** groot **als** de vorige*	this room is **not as** big **as** the previous one
*Corrie is **niet zo** aardig **als** Wim*	Corrie is **not as** nice **as** Wim

2.3 *TOEN, ALS, WANNEER, INDIEN, DAN*   E. 10, 11
2.3.1 *Toen* as adverb

Adverbial *toen* can be used in the sense of:

1. 'then', 'at that moment', 'at that time', 'in those days' (in the past)
2. 'then', 'after that' (in the past)

in de 18e eeuw waren er nog geen treinen	in the 18th century there were no trains
toen reisde men nog per postkoets (sense 1)	in those days one used to travel by mail-coach

eerst parkeerde hij zijn auto,	first he parked his car,
toen liep hij naar de voordeur,	then he walked to the front door,
toen pakte hij zijn sleutel uit zijn tas,	then he took his key out of his bag,
toen maakte hij de deur open (sense 2)	then he opened the door

2.3.2 *Dan* as adverb   E. 11

Adverbial *dan* can be used in four different senses:

1. 'then', 'at that moment' (in the future)
2. 'then', 'after that' (in the future)
3. 'then', 'after that' (in the case of habitual actions, including in the past)
4. 'in that case' (conditional)

in de 21e eeuw reis je niet meer per trein	in the 21st century you won't travel by train anymore
dan ga je per raket naar je werk (sense 1)	then you'll go to work by rocket
ik moet morgen eerst drie uur werken,	tomorrow I first of all have to work for three hours,
dan ga ik naar Utrecht	then I'm going to Utrecht
en dan reis ik 's avonds weer terug	and then I'll travel back to Amsterdam
naar Amsterdam (sense 2)	in the evening
eerst parkeerde hij zijn auto,	first he would park his car,
dan liep hij altijd naar de voordeur,	then he used to walk to the front door,
dan pakte hij altijd zijn sleutel uit zijn tas	then he used to take the key out of his bag,
dan maakte hij de deur open (sense 3)	then he used to open the door
ben je ziek?	are you ill?
dan kun je beter in bed blijven! (sense 4)	then you'd better stay in bed

2.3.3 *Toen* as conjunction

E. 13, 14

When *toen* functions as a conjunction it means 'when', 'at the moment when', 'at the time that' (in the past):

toen de voorzitter uitgesproken was,	when the chairman was finished talking
nam de secretaris het woord	the secretary took over
toen Kees binnen kwam,	when Kees came in
stond Anneke op en liep de kamer uit	Anneke stood up and left the room

2.3.4 *Dan* as conjunction

E. 3

Dan used as a conjunction has a comparative meaning, as in sentences like:

Karel is groter dan Piet	Karel is taller than Piet
hij schrijft beter dan hij schildert	he writes better than he paints

2.3.5 *Als/wanneer* as conjunctions

E. 12

As conjunctions *als* and *wanneer* can be used in three senses:

1. 'when', 'at the moment when', 'at the time that' (in the past or future)
2. 'whenever', 'each time that' (in the case of habitual actions, including in the past)
3. 'if', 'in case' (= *indien*) (conditional)

als de voorzitter uitgesproken is,	when the chairman has finished talking,
kan de secretaris het woord krijgen (sense 1)	the secretary can take over
als Kees straks binnenkomt,	when Kees comes in,
moet je opstaan	you must stand up
en hem feliciteren met zijn verjaardag (sense 1)	and wish him many happy returns
vroeger werkte ik op een fabriek	I used to work at a factory
als ik 's morgens binnenkwam,	when I went in in the morning
stopte ik eerst mijn kaart in de prikklok	I used first to clock in
pas daarna ging ik aan het werk	only then did I start working
en als mijn baas mijn werk gecontroleerd had	and when my boss had checked my work
en weer naar zijn kantoor was gegaan,	and gone back to his office
ging ik naar het toilet	I would go to the toilet
om een sigaret te roken (sense 2)	for a cigarette
in een opera zijn ze altijd aan het zingen	in an opera they're always singing
als ze een brief krijgen,	when they get a letter,
als ze een aardig meisje ontmoeten,	when they meet a nice girl,
zelfs als ze doodgaan! (sense 2)	even when they die!

als je erg ziek bent,	If you're very ill
moet je de dokter bellen (sense 3)	you must phone the doctor
als je geen rijbewijs hebt,	if you do not have a driving licence
mag je niet autorijden (sense 3)	you cannot drive a car

2.3.6 Comparative use of the conjunction *als* E. 4, 5

Als used as a conjunction has a comparative meaning in sentences like:

Kees is net zo groot als Piet	Kees is just as tall as Piet
Jaap is net als Kees:	Jaap's just like Kees:
hij houdt ook niet van opera	he doesn't like opera either

2.3.7 Summarising remarks

1. *Toen* always refers to the past, both as adverb and conjunction.
2. When *dan, als* and *wanneer* are used to refer to the past, habitual action is always involved.

3 FURTHER REMARKS

(1.7) *dat viel wel mee*	it wasn't as bad as we had expected

Meevallen means 'the situation is better than was expected':

dat valt me van hem mee	he's done better than I had expected

The opposite is *tegenvallen:*

dat valt me van hem tegen	he's done worse than I expected
(1.19) *weet je wel*	you know
(1.22) *hoe bevalt die?*	how do you like it?

Bevallen literally means 'to please', so in Dutch the subject noun refers to the object of the liking. Note the following example:

de badkamer (singular) *in dit nieuwe*	I like the bathroom in this new house,
huis bevalt (singular) *me wel, maar*	but I don't like the bedrooms at all
de slaapkamers (plural) *bevallen me*	
helemaal niet	
(1.24) *en alles blijft veel schoner*	and everything remains much cleaner
erg schoon	very clean
veel schoner	much cleaner
(1.27) *ze zijn **dol op** de lift*	they love the lift
*ze zijn **dol op** chocola*	they're crazy about chocolate
(1.28) *o, moet je horen*	

Moet je horen introduces a statement or a question and is meant to draw attention. It means something like 'listen', 'listen to this', or simply 'by the way'.

(1.39) *deze kamer is **een stuk** groter*	this room is **a lot** larger
dan jullie vorige	than your last one

(1.70) *dat scheelt nog in de benzinekosten*	it makes a difference in petrol costs
(1.44) *wat kleiner*	somewhat smaller
(1.40) *dat lijkt maar zo*	it only seems so (E. 7)
(1.46) *die van Corrie is iets groter*	Corrie's is a little bit larger
(1.72) *Jaap is niet voor niets boekhouder*	Jaap is not an accountant for nothing
(1.68) *bij de huur is de verwarming inbegrepen*	the heating is included in the rent

LESSON 22

1 SUMMARY OF THE DIALOGUE

Anneke and John visit Kees. They have a drink and John tells about his visit to the palace that morning. Later Anneke's mother phones. She wants Anneke to come home because there is a friend there waiting for her.

Pay attention to sentences like: – *ze zegt dat er bezoek voor je is*
(a subclause with *dat*)
– *ze vraagt of je naar huis gaat*
(indirect question)

2 GRAMMAR

2.1 SUBCLAUSES INTRODUCED BY *DAT*   E. 1, 3, 6–8

A speaker may report a statement in two ways:

1. by means of a quotation (direct)
2. by means of a subclause with *dat* (indirect)

direct	indirect
ze zegt: 'Ik ben ziek'	*ze zegt dat ze ziek is*
ze zei: 'Ik ben ziek'	*ze zei dat ze ziek was*
ze zegt: 'Ik ben ziek geweest'	*ze zegt dat ze ziek geweest is*
ze zei: 'Ik ben ziek geweest'	*ze zei dat ze ziek geweest was*
John zit net te vertellen dat hij in het paleis geweest is (line 23)	John's just saying that he's been inside the palace
het weerbericht zei dat het zou gaan onweren (1.64)	the weather forecast said there would be thunder

Not only verbs of saying can be followed by *dat*-clauses. Just like in English, there are lots of other cases where you can use them.

*ik geloof ook **dat** het alleen 's zomers maar zo is* (1.28)	I think it's only the case in the summer
*het spijt me **dat** ik nu al weg moet* (1.69)	I'm sorry that I have to be off already
*ik heb altijd gedacht **dat** De Keyser het gebouwd heeft* (1.35)	I always thought that De Keyser was the architect
*ik begrijp best **dat** je naar huis moet* (E. 8)	I understand very well that you have to go home
*wat jammer **dat** je weg moet* (E. 12)	what a shame that you have to go

Pay attention to the word order in the subclause (see also the exercises in lesson 23).

119

LESSON 22

2.2 THE INDIRECT QUESTION

A question, too, may be asked in two ways: either directly, or indirectly by means of a sub-clause. The indirect question may be subdivided in two.

2.2.1 Indirect questions which are introduced by a question word

If we start out from a direct question which begins with a question word, and turn it into an indirect question, this indirect question is introduced by the same question word as the direct question.

direct	indirect
hoe laat ben je thuis gekomen?	*vertel me eens **hoe** laat je thuisgekomen bent*
wie heeft dat boek geschreven?	*ik wil graag weten **wie** dat boek geschreven heeft*
wanneer ga je weg?	*hij vraagt **wanneer** je weg gaat*

2.2.2 Indirect questions introduced by *of*   E. 2

Questions which in their direct form do not begin with a question word are introduced by the conjunction *of* in their indirect form (English: 'whether'/'if').

direct	indirect
is dit de Hoofdweg?	*weet u misschien of dit de Hoofdweg is?*
gaat Kees naar de film?	*weet je of Kees naar de film gaat?*
kom je meteen thuis, Anneke?	*Anneke, je moeder vraagt of je meteen thuiskomt*

(see also the exercises in lesson 23)

2.3 *LOPEN, ZITTEN, STAAN, LIGGEN, HANGEN* + *TE* + INFINITIVE   E. 17

This construction indicates whether the subject is walking, sitting, standing, lying or hanging at the moment of the action.

ik loop te zingen	I am singing
hij zit te lachen	he is laughing
hij staat te kijken	he is looking
ze liggen te lezen	they are reading
de was hangt te drogen	the washing is drying
John zit net te vertellen . . . (1.23)	John is just saying . . .
je loopt je er echt niet te vervelen (1.31)	you won't be bored over there

2.4 REFLEXIVE VERBS

E. 13–15

A reflexive verb is a verb which is accompanied by a reflexive pronoun (see lesson 3, section 2.1.2). The reflexive pronouns are:

(ik	*vergis)*	*me*
(jij	*vergist)*	*je*
(u	*vergist)*	*u/zich*
(hij	*vergist)*	*zich*
(ze	*vergist)*	*zich*
(wij	*vergissen)*	*ons*
(jullie	*vergissen)*	*je*
(u	*vergist)*	*u/zich*
(ze	*vergissen)*	*zich*

A number of verbs are always accompanied by a reflexive pronoun, for example:

zich vergissen	to make a mistake
zich haasten	to hurry
zich afvragen	to wonder
zich vervelen	to feel bored
dus die man heeft zich niet vergist (1.41)	so the man wasn't wrong
dus je begrijpt, ik moet me wel haasten (1.60)	so you understand, I must get a move on

Some verbs may occur both with and without a reflexive pronoun. E.g.

zich wassen	to wash oneself
zich helpen	to help oneself
Els wast zich om 7 uur	Els gets washed at 7 o'clock
Jaap wast zijn sokken	Jaap is washing his socks

Only in these cases can *zelf* be added to the reflexive pronoun in order to express (contrastive) emphasis. *Zelf* cannot be added to the inherently reflexive verbs like *zich vergissen, zich haasten* etc.

Els wast eerst zichzelf en daarna de kinderen	first Els gets washed herself and then she washes the children
je moet eerst andere mensen helpen en pas daarna jezelf	first you must help other people and only then may you help yourself

2.5 THE PASSIVE PERFECT

E. 9, 10

The passive of a sentence in the perfect is formed only by means of the perfect tense auxiliary *zijn*. No past participle of the passive auxiliary is used. See also appendix B2.

active	passive
present tense: *ze wassen de patiënten*	*de patiënten worden gewassen*
simple past: *ze wasten de patiënten*	*de patiënten werden gewassen*
perfect tense: *ze hebben de patiënten gewassen*	*de patiënten zijn gewassen*

ik	*ben*	*gewassen*
je	*bent*	*gewassen*
u	*bent*	*gewassen*
hij	*is*	*gewassen*
ze	*is*	*gewassen*
het	*is*	*gewassen*
we	*zijn*	*gewassen*
jullie	*zijn*	*gewassen*
u	*bent*	*gewassen*
ze	*zijn*	*gewassen*

3   FURTHER REMARKS

(1.2) *bier? sherry? iets sterkers?*   beer? sherry? something stronger?

(1.18) *niets bijzonders*   nothing special

The construction *x* + **adjective** + *s* in which x is a word denoting quantity (e.g. *iets, wat, veel, een heleboel, allerlei*) means: *iets (wat) dat . . .* (adjective) *is.* Thus *iets sterkers = iets dat sterker is.*

een heleboel moois	a lot of beautiful things
veel goeds	a lot of good
iets duurs	something expensive
iets fris (1.3)	a soft drink

N.B. Adjectives ending in *-s* do not get an extra *–s: iets fris.*

The adjective may be a comparative: *iets sterkers.*

(E. 4)

(1.5) *kom nou, je kunt toch wel wat drinken!*   come on, you can have something to drink

(1.6) *nee, echt niet*   no, really

(1.18) *wat dacht je!*   of course

(1.24) *hoe heb je dat voor elkaar gekregen?* how did you manage that?

voor elkaar krijgen   to fix, to manage

(1.29) *is het de moeite waard?*   is it worth while?

de moeite waard zijn   to be worth while

(1.36) *of stond die gids ons iets wijs te maken?*   or was that guide kidding us?

iemand iets wijs maken   to kid, to have a person believe something

(1.37) *volgens mij is het Van Campen*   in my opinion it was Van Campen

(1.44) *lang niet alle zalen waren open*

lang niet alle   by no means all rooms were open

1.45) *maar ik heb toch **een aardige indruk** gekregen* — but I still got **a nice impression**

1.67) *wat aardig van je!* — how nice of you!

1.49) *ik kom eraan* — I'm coming

1.58) *die maar een uurtje tijd heeft* — who has got only one hour to spare

1.59) *we hebben elkaar al in geen jaren gezien* — we haven't seen each other for years

al in geen jaren = al jaren niet — not for years

LESSON 23

LESSON 23

1 SUMMARY OF THE DIALOGUE

Kees pays a visit to John, who is ill. He makes a phone call to cancel an appointment which John had made. He doesn't know the number, but he finds out by phoning the telephone information service.

Pay attention to: – the auxiliary *zou*
– subclauses introduced by *dat* and indirect questions

2 GRAMMAR

2.1 *ZOU* AND *WOU* IN POLITE REQUESTS   E. 12

zou ik dan zijn secretaresse even kunnen spreken (line 59)
could I have a word with his secretary in that case, please?
zou u aan de heer Meyboom willen doorgeven, dat meneer King ziek is? (1.65)
could you inform Mr Meyboom that Mr King is ill, please?
ik wou graag een nummer in Hilversum hebben (1.41)
I would like a number in Hilversum, please

To make requests more polite one can add the auxiliary *zou*. Strictly speaking *zou* is a past tense form (of the verb *zullen*), but when used in requests it simply makes the request more polite. In such cases it is equivalent to the English word 'could'. Like English 'could' Dutch *zou* has many other meanings and functions.

Roughly speaking, there are six common ways of expressing a request, either with *ik* (1, 2 and 3) or with *u/je* (4, 5 and 6).

1. A statement consisting of *ik* + a form of the verb *willen* + a main verb (if necessary). The past tense of *willen* has two forms, *wilde(n)* and *wou(den)*. These forms also make the request more polite. The following examples are ordered from more straightforward to more polite:

ik wil een kopje koffie (*hebben*)
*ik wil **graag** een kopje koffie*
*ik **wilde** graag een kopje koffie*
*ik **wou** graag een kopje koffie*
*ik **zou** graag een kopje koffie **willen***

ik wil weten waar het station is
*ik wil **graag** weten waar het station is*
*ik **wilde** graag weten waar het station is*
*ik **wou** graag weten waar het station is*
*ik **zou** graag **willen** weten waar het station is*

2. A question with *mogen* in combination with *ik:*

mag ik een kopje koffie (hebben)?
*mag ik een kopje koffie **alstublieft?***
*zou ik een kopje koffie **mogen alstublieft?***

mag ik je pen even lenen?
*mag ik je pen **misschien** even lenen?*
*zou ik je pen misschien even **mogen** lenen?*

3. A question with *kunnen* in combination with *ik:*

kan ik je pen even lenen?
*kan ik je pen **misschien** even lenen?*
*zou ik je pen misschien even **kunnen** lenen?*

4. A question with *hebben* + *u/je:*

heb jij een kopje koffie voor me?
*heb jij **misschien** een kopje koffie voor me?*
*zou jij misschien een kopje koffie voor me **hebben?***

5. A question with *willen* + *u/je:*

wil je me even helpen?
*wil je me misschien even helpen **alsjeblieft?***
*wil je me **misschien** even helpen?*
*zou je me even **willen** helpen alsjeblieft?*
*zou je me misschien even **willen** helpen?*

6. The most polite request pattern with *u/je* is that which takes the auxiliary *kunnen:*

kunt u me zeggen waar het station is?
*kunt u me **misschien** zeggen waar het station is?*
*zou u me misschien **kunnen** zeggen waar het station is?*

kun je me een kopje koffie geven?
*zou je me een kopje koffie **kunnen** geven?*

kun je mij je pen even lenen?
*kun je mij je pen **misschien** even lenen?*
*kun je mij je pen **alsjeblieft** even lenen?*
***zou** je mij je pen misschien even **kunnen** lenen?*

3   FURTHER REMARKS

3.1   MAKING A TELEPHONE CALL

Here is some advice concerning making phone calls.
If the telephone rings, you pick up the receiver and say your name (not *hallo*):

met juffrouw Visser (1.61)	Miss Visser speaking
u spreekt met de firma De Graaff,	'firma De Graaff', good afternoon
goedemiddag	

The person making the call then says their name, also by means of (*u spreekt*) *met* . . .

u spreekt met Bergsma
met Bergsma (1.62)

If the person you are speaking to is not the one you want to speak to, you say:

kan ik . . . (name) *even spreken?*	I would like to talk to . . .

When you phone a firm or institution which has many extensions, you say:

kunt u me doorverbinden met . . . (name)	could you put me through to . . .
(1.56)	

The switchboard operator then says:

jazeker, ik verbind u door (1.60)	certainly, Ill put you through

geen gehoor	no answer
in gesprek (1.54)	(number) engaged
het netnummer	number of the telephone district
het abonneenummer	number of the individual telephone
ik wou graag een nummer in Hilversum	I would like to have a number in Hilversum
hebben (1.41)	
een ogenblikje, alstublieft (1.74)	just a moment, please
met wie spreek ik?	who is speaking?

3.2 MISCELLANEOUS REMARKS

(1.21) *dan bel ik inlichtingen wel even*   in that case I'll phone the information service
of the *telefoondienst*

(1.11/16) If an auxiliary occurs twice in one sentence (whether accompanied by an infinitive or a past participle), it is often left out the second time. The same goes for the subject if it occurs twice.

hij heeft me wat tabletten gegeven en (hij heeft) gezegd . . . (1.16–17)

wil je die man voor me opbellen en (wil je) hem zeggen dat . . . (1.16–17)

(1.67) *het spijt hem **erg***   he is **very** sorry

       *het spijt me **verschrikkelijk***   I am **terribly** sorry

       *het spijt me **helemaal niet***   I am **not** sorry **at all**

LESSON 24

1 SUMMARY OF THE DIALOGUE

Anneke happens to meet John in a bookshop. He says that he is going back to Britain. They take a walk together and Anneke hears all about the reason for John's departure.

Pay attention to: – sentences with a double infinitive
– relative subclauses
– diminutives

2 GRAMMAR

2.1 THE DOUBLE INFINITIVE CONSTRUCTION   E. 5–8

A verb phrase consisting of the PV of an auxiliary plus an infinitive (without *te*)in the present tense, e.g. *ik kan de brief niet lezen* ('I cannot read the letter') takes on a particular form in the perfect. The PV of an auxiliary does not become a past participle, as one might expect, but an **infinitive.** This infinitive precedes the other infinitive (see also lesson 18, E. 10):

ik heb de brief niet kunnen lezen   I could not read the letter

Here are some more examples:

ik laat mijn auto wassen	I have my car washed
ik heb mijn auto laten wassen	I had my car washed
ik kom zaterdag eten	I'm coming for dinner on Saturday
ik ben zaterdag komen eten	I came for dinner on Saturday
hij mag geen bier drinken	he's not allowed to drink any beer
hij heeft geen bier mogen drinken	he wasn't allowed to drink any beer
we willen Anneke niet uitnodigen	we don't want to invite Anneke
we hebben Anneke niet willen uitnodigen	we didn't want to invite Anneke
je moet de auto wassen	you have to wash the car
je had de auto moeten wassen	you should have washed the car
heeft de juffrouw al iets laten zien? (line 9)	has the assistant shown you anything?
ze heeft me zelf laten zoeken (1.10)	she let me look myself
ik had haar net willen roepen (1.11)	I was going to call her just now

2.2 RELATIVE CLAUSES   E. 1–4

Relative clauses may be introduced by a number of relatives.

2.2.1 *Die* and *dat*

Often relative clauses are introduced by *die* or *dat*. This was treated in lesson 18.
Here are some more examples:

hier is de kamer die ik voor u heb	here is the room that I have for you
hier is het behang dat ik uitgezocht heb	here is the wallpaper that I chose
hier staan de meubels die u krijgt	here is the furniture that you will get

2.2.2 *Waar*

If the relative is the object of a preposition in the same relative clause, it takes the form *waar*
(cf. lesson 14, section 2.1.1).

*het TV-programma **waar** we **naar** gekeken hebben, was erg interessant*	the TV-programme we were watching was very interesting
*het eten **waar** ik het meest **van** houd, is kip met rijst*	the food I like best is chicken with rice
*het radioprogramma **waar** Anneke elke dag **naar** luistert, is de ochtendgymnastiek*	the radio programme that Anneke listens to every day is the morning keep-fit programme
*de film **waar** we niet **naar** hoeven te kijken, heet 'Spelen met vuur'*	the film that we don't need to watch is called 'Spelen met vuur'
*de vergadering **waar** John morgen **naartoe** moet, begint om 10 uur*	the meeting that John has to go to tomorrow begins at 10 o'clock
*Engeland is het land **waar** John King **vandaan** komt*	England is the country where John King comes from

The preposition may immediately follow *waar,* but may also come at the end of the
dependent clause, before the verb.

*ik weet niet **waarover** jullie praten*
*ik weet niet **waar** jullie **over** praten*

*ik weet niet **waarover** jullie gisteren gepraat hebben*
*ik weet niet **waar** jullie gisteren **over** gepraat hebben*

*ik weet niet **waarover** jullie morgen gaan praten*
*ik weet niet **waar** jullie morgen **over** gaan praten*

*kunt u me zeggen **waarmee** ik u kan helpen?*
*ik weet nog niet **waar** ik in de vakantie **naartoe/heen** ga*
*ik kan niet zien **waar** hij **naar** kijkt*
*het is een buitenlander, maar ik weet niet **waar** hij **vandaan** komt*
*ik wil haar iets lekkers geven, maar ik weet niet **waar** ze **van** houdt*

ik wil haar graag iets geven	I'd like to give her something
waar *ze iets* **aan** *heeft* (1.25)	that is of some use to her
ik heb een aanbieding gekregen	I have had an offer from the newspaper
van de krant **waar** *ik* **voor** *werk* (1.30)	that I work for
de man **waar** *alles* **om** *draaide op de*	the man who was the key figure in the
afdeling . . . zou . . . met pensioen gaan	department was going to retire
(1.48)	

2.3 DIMINUTIVES

A diminutive is a special form of a noun that generally indicates that what is referred to is either small in size (literally or figuratively), not too important, or the object of affection. Nouns form their diminutives by means of the suffix -*je* with the variations -*tje, -etje, -pje, -kje* depending on the last sound of the noun. Here are some rules for the use of the variations:

-*je*
A noun takes the suffix -*je* if it ends in a voiceless consonant:

kop	– *kopje*
brief	– *briefje*
plaat	– *plaatje* (1.21)
terras	– *terrasje* (1.41)
eind	– *eindje* (1.41)
dag	– *dagje*

-*tje*
A noun takes the suffix -*tje* if it ends in: 1. a vowel (which is often doubled in spelling)
2. a diphthong
3. -*l, -n, -r*, preceded by: a) a long vowel
                                                       b) a diphthong
                                                       c) /ə/

auto	– *autootje* (1)	car
bui	– *buitje* (2)	shower (of rain)
stoel	– *stoeltje* (3a)	chair
telefoon	– *telefoontje* (1.38) (3a)	telephone
jaar	– *jaartje* (3a)	year
trein	– *treintje* (3b)	train
tuin	– *tuintje* (3b)	garden
dochter	– *dochtertje* (1.4) (3c)	daughter

-*etje*
A noun takes the suffix -*etje* if it ends in -**l, -m, -n, -r, -ng,** preceded by a short vowel (-*l, -m, -n, -r*, are doubled).

bal	– balletje	ball
kam	– kammetje	comb
roman	– romannetje (1.13)	novel
ster	– sterretje	star
wandeling	– wandelingetje (1.42)	walk

-pje

A noun takes -pje if it ends in -m preceded by: 1. a long vowel
2. a diphthong
3. /ə/
4. -l
5. -r

bloem	– bloempje (1) (there is also bloemetje meaning 'a bunch of flowers')	flower
geheim	– geheimpje (2)	secret
harem	– harempje (3)	harem
film	– filmpje (4)	film
berm	– bermpje (5)	verge (of a road)

-kje

A noun takes the suffix -kje if it ends in -ing and the last but one syllable is stressed. The -g disappears:

woning – woninkje	flat
ketting – kettinkje	chain
koning – koninkje	king

3   FURTHER REMARKS

(1.1) Anneke, ook op zoek naar een boek?	Anneke, looking for a book too?
op zoek zijn naar iets	to look for something
(1.20) maar Ineke is het vast niet met me eens	but Ineke most likely doesn't agree with me
het eens zijn met	to agree
(1.25) ik wil haar graag iets geven	I'd like to give her something
waar ze iets aan heeft	that is of some use to her
(1.27) hoe komt dat?	how come?
(1.28) ja, nou ja, ik ga weer terug naar Engeland	yeah, that is to say, I'm going back to England
(1.32) dat is natuurlijk een aardige promotie	that is of course quite a promotion
(1.42) ik heb eigenlijk best zin in een wandelingetje	I'd quite like going for a little walk actually

131

(1.45) *heb je trek in een ijsje?*   do you fancy an ice cream?
trek hebben in is only used when food is involved
zin hebben in may also refer to other things

(1.51) *voor zover ik weet tenminste*   as far as I know at least

(1.52) *ik heb me wel eens **stilletjes***   I've sometimes **secretly** wondered if
afgevraagd of ik in aanmerking   I would be considered
zou komen
in aanmerking komen voor   to be considered for

(1.54) *hoe zit het nou?*   here: why don't you come to the point?

(1.57) *hij krijgt vervroegd pensioen*   he's been granted an early retirement

APPENDICES

APPENDIX A   SPELLING

A1. THE SPELLING OF VOWELS

If the last letter of a syllable is a vowel, it is called an **open** syllable; if the last letter of a syllable is a consonant, it is called a **closed** syllable.

1. The spelling of *ie, ou, au, ei, ij, eu, ui, oe* and *y* never changes:

in a closed syllable	in an open syllable
tuin	*tui-nen*
gebouw	*gebou-wen*
blauw	*blau-we*
klein	*klei-ne*
tijd	*tij-den*
deur	*deu-ren*
ziek	*zie-ken*
typ	*ty-pen*

2. **The sounds** $/\alpha/$, $/o/$, $/\varepsilon/$, $/\iota/$, and $/\partial/$ are always written with one letter; the syllable must always be closed:

lat	*lat-ten*	*last*	*las-ten*
kop	*kop-pen*	*rots*	*rot-sen*
tik	*tik-ken*	*kist*	*kis-ten*
pet	*pet-ten*	*rest*	*res-ten*
bus	*bus-sen*	*kust*	*kus-ten*

(exceptions: *la-chen, li-chaam, hè, gô*)
(See note below)

3. In a closed syllable the spelling of the **sounds** /a:/, /o:/, /e:/ and /y:/ is *aa, oo, ee, uu*; in an open syllable *a, o, e, u*.

straat	*stra-ten*	*schaats*	*schaat-sen*
loop	*lo-pen*	*poort*	*poor-ten*
steen	*ste-nen*	*feest*	*fees-ten*
uur	*u-ren*	*buurt*	*buur-ten*

So the **letters** *a, o, u,* are symbols for two different sounds:
for $/\alpha/$ and /a:/ as in *tak* and *taken*
for /o/ and /o:/ as in *bom* and *bomen*
for $/\partial/$ and /y:/ as in *stug* and *spugen*

APPENDIX A

The **letter** *e* is a symbol for three different sounds:
for / ε / as in *spel* and *stel*
for /e:/ as in *spelen* and *stelen*
for /ə/ as in *zitten, kosten, huizenhoog*

The **sound** /ə/ is sometimes spelt as *u*, sometimes as *e*, sometimes as *i*, and sometimes as *ij*:
bus, bussen, nuttig, verrukkelijk, zitten, bijten, twintig, zestig, tijdig, moeilijk, makkelijk, eigenlijk.

Note:
1. If there is one consonant between two vowels and it is not a compound word the syllable boundary is before the consonant (*ch* is regarded as one consonant):

tui-nen	*ty-pen*	*klei-ne*	*be-ter*
tij-den	*boe-ken*	*la-chen*	*va-der*
deu-ren	*zie-ke*	*li-chaam*	*bo-men*

2. If there are two consonants and it is not a compound word, the boundary is between the two consonants (*ng* is regarded as two consonants):

gees-ten	*paar-den*	*bes-te*	*har-ten*
kop-pen	*val-len*	*van-gen*	

A2. TERMS RELATING TO SPELLING AND PRONUNCIATION

de zin	sentence
het woord	word
de lettergreep, de syllabe	syllable
de letter	letter
de klank	sound
de uitspraak	pronunciation
de klemtoon, het accent	stress
de medeklinker, de consonant	consonant
de klinker, de vocaal	vowel
het bastaardwoord, het leenwoord	loanword

het leesteken	punctation mark	
de punt	full stop	.
het vraagteken	question mark	?
het uitroepteken	exclamation mark	!
de komma	comma	,
de dubbele punt	colon	:
de puntkomma, de kommapunt	semicolon	;
de aanhalingstekens	quotation marks	*hij zei: "Dat is niet waar."*
de gedachtenstreep	hyphen	*we geloven - en dat hebben we al eens eerder gezegd - niet dat dat waar is*

het koppelteken	dash	*in- en uitvoer, Noord-Holland*
het deelteken, de trema	diaeresis	*zeeëenden*
het weglatingsteken, de apostroph	apostrophe	*'s ochtends, Frits' fiets*
(tussen) haakjes	(between) brackets	( )
de schuine streep	oblique	/

APPENDIX B VERB CONJUGATION

B1. VERB CONJUGATION - PRESENT TENSE

1. REGULAR CONJUGATION

Some examples of regular verbs follow. Note that if inversion of the *je* form takes place, the verb has no *-t*:

infinitive:	*werken*	*spellen*	*spelen*	*wonen*
sing. 1. *ik*	*werk*	*spel*	*speel*	*woon*
2. *je*	*werkt*	*spelt*	*speelt*	*woont*
u	*werkt*	*spelt*	*speelt*	*woont*
3. *hij*	*werkt*	*spelt*	*speelt*	*woont*
ze	*werkt*	*spelt*	*speelt*	*woont*
het	*werkt*	*spelt*	*speelt*	*woont*
plur. 1. *we*	*werken*	*spellen*	*spelen*	*wonen*
2. *jullie*	*werken*	*spellen*	*spelen*	*wonen*
3. *ze*	*werken*	*spellen*	*spelen*	*wonen*
	werk je	*spel je*	*speel je*	*woon je*

2. REGULAR VERBS WITH *-T* OR *-D* AS STEM-FINAL CONSONANTS

infinitive:	*zitten*	*eten*	*vinden*	*worden*	*braden*
sing. 1. *ik*	*zit*	*eet*	*vind*	*word*	*braad*
2. *je*	*zit*	*eet*	*vindt*	*wordt*	*braadt*
u	*zit*	*eet*	*vindt*	*wordt*	*braadt*
3. *hij*	*zit*	*eet*	*vindt*	*wordt*	*braadt*
ze	*zit*	*eet*	*vindt*	*wordt*	*braadt*
het	*zit*	*eet*	*vindt*	*wordt*	*braadt*
plur. 1. *we*	*zitten*	*eten*	*vinden*	*worden*	*braden*
2. *jullie*	*zitten*	*eten*	*vinden*	*worden*	*braden*
3. *ze*	*zitten*	*eten*	*vinden*	*worden*	*braden*
	zit je	*eet je*	*vind je*	*word je*	*braad je*

N.B. The pronunciation of *word-wordt*, *vind-vindt* and of *braad-braadt* is exactly the same.

3. REGULAR VERBS WITH *F/V* OR *S/Z* AS STEM-FINAL CONSONANTS

Note the difference between the verbs with *-v-* or *-z-* and the verbs with *-ff-* or *-(s)s-* in plural forms (see appendix B2).

infinitive:	*leven*	*straffen*	*reizen*	*missen*	*dansen*
sing. 1. *ik*	leef	straf	reis	mis	dans
2. *je*	leeft	straft	reist	mist	danst
u	leeft	straft	reist	mist	danst
3. *hij*	leeft	straft	reist	mist	danst
ze	leeft	straft	reist	mist	danst
het	leeft	straft	reist	mist	danst
plur. 1. *we*	leven	straffen	reizen	missen	dansen
2. *jullie*	leven	straffen	reizen	missen	dansen
3. *ze*	leven	straffen	reizen	missen	dansen
	leef je	straf je	reis je	mis je	dans je

4. REGULAR VOCALIC VERBS

infinitive:	*zien*	*doen*	*gaan*	*staan*
sing. 1. *ik*	zie	doe	ga	sta
2. *je*	ziet	doet	gaat	staat
u	ziet	doet	gaat	staat
3. *hij*	ziet	doet	gaat	staat
ze	ziet	doet	gaat	staat
het	ziet	doet	gaat	staat
plur. 1. *we*	zien	doen	gaan	staan
2. *jullie*	zien	doen	gaan	staan
3. *ze*	zien	doen	gaan	staan
	zie je	doe je	ga je	sta je

N.B. The pronunciation of *a* in *ga* and *sta* and of *aa* in *gaat* and *staat* is exactly the same (see appendix A1).

5. IRREGULAR VERBS

infinitive:	*willen*	*zullen*	*kunnen*
sing. 1. *ik*	wil	zal	kan
2. *je*	wil + wilt	zal + zult	kan + kunt
u	wil + wilt	zal + zult	kan + kunt
3. *hij*	wil	zal	kan
ze	wil	zal	kan
het	wil	zal	kan
plur. 1. *we*	willen	zullen	kunnen
2. *jullie*	willen	zullen	kunnen
3. *ze*	willen	zullen	kunnen
	wil je	zal je + zul je	kan je + kun je

APPENDIX B

infinitive:	*mogen*	*komen*	*hebben*	*zijn*
sing. 1. *ik*	*mag*	*kom*	*heb*	*ben*
2. *je*	*mag*	*komt*	*hebt*	*bent*
u	*mag*	*komt*	*hebt* + *heeft*	*bent* + *is*
3. *hij*	*mag*	*komt*	*heeft*	*is*
ze	*mag*	*komt*	*heeft*	*is*
het	*mag*	*komt*	*heeft*	*is*
plur. 1. *we*	*mogen*	*komen* *	*hebben*	*zijn*
2. *jullie*	*mogen*	*komen*	*hebben*	*zijn*
3. *ze*	*mogen*	*komen*	*hebben*	*zijn*
	mag je	*kom je*	*heb je*	*ben je*

* Note the pronunciation: not **kommen,** but **komen!**

B2. VERB CONJUGATION - PAST TENSE

In the past and perfect tense we distinguish 1. weak verbs and
2. strong and irregular verbs.

1. WEAK VERBS

– The past tense is formed by adding *te*(*n*) or *de*(*n*)to the stem: *te* or *de* for singular forms and *ten* or *den* for plural forms. The past participle is formed as follows:

$ge + \text{stem} + {}^{t}_{d}$.

– *-d* at the end of a word is always pronounced as *t*.

werken - infinitive   **spellen** - infinitive
werk   - stem   **spel**   - stem

present		past	perfect	
ik	*werk /spel*	*werkte /spelde*	*heb*	*gewerkt/gespeld*
*je**	*werkt /spelt*	*werkte /spelde*	*hebt*	*gewerkt/gespeld*
u	*werkt /spelt*	*werkte /spelde*	*hebt*	*gewerkt/gespeld*
hij	*werkt /spelt*	*werkte /spelde*	*heeft*	*gewerkt/gespeld*
ze	*werkt /spelt*	*werkte /spelde*	*heeft*	*gewerkt/gespeld*
het	*werkt /spelt*	*werkte /spelde*	*heeft*	*gewerkt/gespeld*
we	*werken/spellen*	*werkten/spelden*	*hebben*	*gewerkt/gespeld*
jullie	*werken/spellen*	*werkten/spelden*	*hebben*	*gewerkt/gespeld*
ze	*werken/spellen*	*werkten/spelden*	*hebben*	*gewerkt/gespeld*

* Note that there is no *t* if the order is reversed: *werk je, spel je.*

SPELLING

Group I: final stem-consonant is *k, p,* or *ch*

present:	ik werk	waak	stap	juich	scherp
	je werkt	waakt	stapt	juicht	scherpt
	we werken	waken	stappen	juichen	scherpen
perfect:	ik heb gewerkt	gewaakt	gestapt	gejuicht	gescherpt
past :	ik werkte	waakte	stapte	juichte	scherpte

Group IIa: final stem consonant is *f* or *s*; in the infinitive or in plural forms: *-v-*
- cons. +*v-*
-z-
- cons. +*z-*

present:	ik leef	reis	durf	golf	peins	omhels
	je leeft	reist	durft	golft	peinst	omhelst
	we leven	reizen	durven	golven	peinzen	omhelzen
perfect:	ik heb geleefd	gereisd	gedurfd	gegolfd	gepeinsd	omhelsd
past :	ik leefde	reisde	durfde	golfde	peinsde	omhelsde

Group IIb: final stem-consonant is *f* or *s*; in the infinitive or in plural forms: *-ff-*
-s-
-cons.+s-

present:	ik straf	mis	dans	kruis
	je straft	mist	danst	kruist
	we straffen	missen	dansen	kruisen
perfect :	ik heb gestraft	gemist	gedanst	gekruist
past :	ik strafte	miste	danste	kruiste

Group III: final stem-consonant is *t*

present:	ik wacht	praat	zet
	je wacht	praat	zet
	we wachten	praten	zetten
perfect :	ik heb gewacht	gepraat	gezet
past :	ik wachtte	praatte	zette

Group IV: final stem-consonant is *d*

present:	ik red	baad	antwoord
	je redt	baadt	antwoordt
	we redden	baden	antwoorden
perfect :	ik heb gered	gebaad	geantwoord
past :	ik redde	baadde	antwoordde

Group V: final stem-consonant is not *k, p, ch, f, s, t, d*

present:	ik leg	aai	wil	voel
	je legt	aait	wilt	voelt
	we leggen	aaien	willen	voelen
perfect :	ik heb gelegd	geaaid	gewild	gevoeld
past :	ik legde	aaide	wilde	voelde

2. STRONG AND IRREGULAR VERBS

Unlike weak verbs, strong verbs do not add a suffix (*-de* or *-te*) to the stem in the past tense. The principal stem-vowel changes in the past tense and sometimes also in the past participle. The past participle generally ends in *-(e)n*.

present				past			participle
ik	vind	doe	neem	vond	deed	nam	gevonden
je*	vindt	doet	neemt	vond	deed	nam	gedaan
u	vindt	doet	neemt	vond	deed	nam	genomen
hij	vindt	doet	neemt	vond	deed	nam	
ze	vindt	doet	neemt	vond	deed	nam	
het	vindt	doet	neemt	vond	deed	nam	
we	vinden	doen	nemen	vonden	deden	namen	
jullie	vinden	doen	nemen	vonden	deden	namen	
ze	vinden	doen	nemen	vonden	deden	namen	

Note the difference in pronunciation of the vowel *a* in *nam* and *namen*.

* Note that there is no *t* if the order is reserved: *vind je, doe je, neem je*.

A list of the most useful strong and irregular verbs is given below. Note that the word *is* before the past participle indicates that *zijn* is used in the perfect tense rather than *hebben;* the word *is* in parenthesis indicates that *zijn* is used in the perfect tense when destination is specified or when used intransitively.

Strong verbs

bijten	beet, beten	gebeten	to bite
blijven	bleef, bleven	is gebleven	to stay
glijden	gleed, gleden	is gegleden	to slide
kijken	keek, keken	gekeken	to look
krijgen	kreeg, kregen	gekregen	to get
lijken	leek, leken	geleken	to look like
rijden	reed, reden	(is) gereden	to ride
rijzen	rees, rezen	is gerezen	to rise
schijnen	scheen, schenen	geschenen	to appear, shine

schrijven	schreef, schreven	geschreven	to write
snijden	sneed, sneden	gesneden	to cut
stijgen	steeg, stegen	is gestegen	to rise
verdwijnen	verdween, verdwenen	is verdwenen	to disappear
vermijden	vermeed, vermeden	vermeden	to avoid
wijzen	wees, wezen	gewezen	to point out
zwijgen	zweeg, zwegen	gezwegen	to be silent
bieden	bood, boden	geboden	to offer
gieten	goot, goten	gegoten	to pour, cast
kiezen	koos, kozen	gekozen	to choose
schieten	schoot, schoten	geschoten	to shoot
verliezen	verloor, verloren	verloren	to lose
vliegen	vloog, vlogen	(is) gevlogen	to fly
vriezen	vroor, (vroren)	gevroren	to freeze
verbieden	verbood, verboden	verboden	to forbid
buigen	boog, bogen	gebogen	to bend
druipen	droop, dropen	(is) gedropen	to drip
fluiten	floot, floten	gefloten	to whistle
kruipen	kroop, kropen	(is) gekropen	to crawl
ruiken	rook, roken	geroken	to smell
schuiven	schoof, schoven	geschoven	to push
sluiten	sloot, sloten	gesloten	to close
binden	bond, bonden	gebonden	to tie
drinken	dronk, dronken	gedronken	to drink
beginnen	begon, begonnen	is begonnen	to begin
klinken	klonk, klonken	geklonken	to sound
krimpen	kromp, krompen	is gekrompen	to shrink
springen	sprong, sprongen	(is) gesprongen	to jump
vinden	vond, vonden	gevonden	to find
winnen	won, wonnen	gewonnen	to win
zingen	zong, zongen	gezongen	to sing
zinken	zonk, zonken	is gezonken	to sink
gelden	gold, golden	gegolden	to be valid
schenken	schonk, schonken	geschonken	to give, pour
trekken	trok, trokken	getrokken	to pull
zenden	zond, zonden	gezonden	to send
zwemmen	zwom, zwommen	(is) gezwommen	to swim
nemen	nam, namen	genomen	to take
breken	brak, braken	(is) gebroken	to break
komen	kwam, kwamen	is gekomen	to come

spreken	*sprak, spraken*	*gesproken*	to speak
stelen	*stal, stalen*	*gestolen*	to steal
geven	*gaf, gaven*	*gegeven*	to give
eten	*at, aten*	*gegeten*	to eat
lezen	*las, lazen*	*gelezen*	to read
treden	*trad, traden*	*is getreden*	to step
vergeten	*vergat, vergaten*	*vergeten*	to forget
bidden	*bad, baden*	*gebeden*	to pray
liggen	*lag, lagen*	*gelegen*	to lie
zitten	*zat, zaten*	*gezeten*	to sit
blazen	*blies, bliezen*	*geblazen*	to blow (breath)
houden	*hield, hielden*	*gehouden*	to hold
laten	*liet, lieten*	*gelaten*	to let
lopen	*liep, liepen*	*(is) gelopen*	to walk, run
roepen	*riep, riepen*	*geroepen*	to call
slapen	*sliep, sliepen*	*geslapen*	to sleep
vallen	*viel, vielen*	*is gevallen*	to fall
bederven	*bedierf, bedierven*	*(is) bedorven*	to spoil, to go bad
helpen	*hielp, hielpen*	*geholpen*	to help
scheppen	*schiep, schiepen*	*geschapen*	to create
sterven	*stierf, stierven*	*is gestorven*	to die
werpen	*wierp, wierpen*	*geworpen*	to throw
dragen	*droeg, droegen*	*gedragen*	to wear, carry
graven	*groef, groeven*	*gegraven*	to dig
slaan	*sloeg, sloegen*	*geslagen*	to strike
varen	*voer, voeren*	*(is) gevaren*	to sail
gaan	*ging, gingen*	*is gegaan*	to go
hangen	*hing, hingen*	*gehangen*	to hang
vangen	*ving, vingen*	*gevangen*	to catch
bewegen	*bewoog, bewogen*	*bewogen*	to move
scheren	*schoor, schoren*	*geschoren*	to shave
wegen	*woog, wogen*	*gewogen*	to weigh
zweren	*zwoer, zwoeren*	*gezworen*	to swear
worden	*werd, werden*	*is geworden*	to become

Irregular verbs

bakken	*bakte, bakten*	*gebakken*	to bake, fry
braden	*braadde, braadden*	*gebraden*	to roast

brengen	*bracht, brachten*	*gebracht*	to bring
denken	*dacht, dachten*	*gedacht*	to think
doen	*deed, deden*	*gedaan*	to do
hebben	*had, hadden*	*gehad*	to have
heten	*heette, heetten*	*geheten*	to be called
jagen	*jaagde, jaagden*	*gejaagd*	to chase
	joeg, joegen		
kopen	*kocht, kochten*	*gekocht*	to buy
kunnen	*kon, konden*	*gekund*	to be able
lachen	*lachte, lachten*	*gelachen*	to laugh
moeten	*moest, moesten*	*gemoeten*	to have to
mogen	*mocht, mochten*	*gemogen*	to be permitted to
plegen	*placht, plachten*		to be accustomed to
			past tense: used to
scheiden	*scheidde, scheidden*	*gescheiden*	to separate
staan	*stond, stonden*	*gestaan*	to stand
vouwen	*vouwde, vouwden*	*gevouwen*	to fold
vragen	*vroeg, vroegen*	*gevraagd*	to ask
	vraagde, vraagden		
waaien	*waaide, waaiden*	*gewaaid*	to blow
	woei, woeien		
wassen	*waste, wasten*	*gewassen*	to wash
weten	*wist, wisten*	*geweten*	to know
willen	*wilde, wilden*	*gewild*	to want to
	wou, wouden		
zeggen	*zei, zeiden*	*gezegd*	to say
zien	*zag, zagen*	*gezien*	to see
zijn	*was, waren*	*geweest*	to be
zoeken	*zocht, zochten*	*gezocht*	to look for
zullen	*zou, zouden*		

3. PERFECT AND PAST PERFECT

perfect:

ik	*heb*	*gewerkt*
je	*hebt*	*gewerkt*
u	*hebt*	*gewerkt*
hij	*heeft*	*gewerkt*
ze	*heeft*	*gewerkt*
het	*heeft*	*gewerkt*
we	*hebben*	*gewerkt*
jullie	*hebben*	*gewerkt*
ze	*hebben*	*gewerkt*

past perfect:

ik	*had*	*gewerkt*
je	*had*	*gewerkt*
u	*had*	*gewerkt*
hij	*had*	*gewerkt*
ze	*had*	*gewerkt*
het	*had*	*gewerkt*
we	*hadden*	*gewerkt*
jullie	*hadden*	*gewerkt*
ze	*hadden*	*gewerkt*

APPENDIX B

perfect:				past perfect:		
ik	ben	gegaan		ik	was	gegaan
je	bent	gegaan		je	was	gegaan
u	bent	gegaan		u	was	gegaan
hij	is	gegaan		hij	was	gegaan
ze	is	gegaan		ze	was	gegaan
het	is	gegaan		het	was	gegaan
we	zijn	gegaan		we	waren	gegaan
jullie	zijn	gegaan		jullie	waren	gegaan
ze	zijn	gegaan		ze	waren	gegaan

4. THE AUXILIARIES *HEBBEN* AND *ZIJN*

It is apparent from the two examples in the previous section that the auxiliary going with **werken** is **hebben,** and that the auxiliary going with **gaan** is **zijn.** Now the question is: which verbs go together with **hebben,** and which go with **zijn**?

4.1 Most verbs go with **hebben**; it is therefore difficult to list them.

4.2 A smaller group of verbs have **zijn** as their auxiliary. Those that are used most frequently are listed below:

infinitive	perfect/past perfect
zijn	ik ben/was geweest
gaan	ik ben/was gegaan
komen	ik ben/was gekomen
blijven	ik ben/was gebleven
worden	ik ben/was geworden
vallen	ik ben/was gevallen
beginnen	ik ben/was begonnen
groeien	ik ben/was gegroeid
sterven	ik ben/was gestorven
rijzen	ik ben/was gerezen
verdwijnen	ik ben/was verdwenen
zinken	ik ben/was gezonken

4.3 Verbs that express movement, such as *lopen, fietsen, reizen, wandelen, zwemmen, varen, vliegen* etc. may be inflected with both **hebben** and **zijn**. The rule is as follows: if aim or direction is explicitly mentioned (*naar* + NP) you use **zijn**; if not you use **hebben**.

*ik ben **naar** huis gefietst*	*ik heb drie uur lang gefietst*
*ik ben **naar** Rotterdam gereden*	*ik heb de hele dag gereden*
*ik ben er gisteren **naartoe** gevlogen*	*ik heb 1½ uur gevlogen*

B3. SURVEY OF TENSES

Given below is a survey of the four tenses in transitive and intransitive verbs:

1 = present
2 = simple past
3 = perfect
4 = past perfect

transitive + active
1. *Kees koopt een auto*
2. *Kees kocht een auto*
3. *Kees heeft een auto gekocht*
4. *Kees had een auto gekocht*

transitive + passive
1. *Kees z'n auto wordt gewassen (door Wim, elke zaterdagmiddag)*
2. *Kees z'n auto werd gewassen*
3. *Kees z'n auto is gewassen*
4. *Kees z'n auto was gewassen*

intransitive + active
1. *de mensen lachen hard om de clown*
2. *de mensen lachten hard om de clown*
3. *de mensen hebben hard om de clown gelachen*
4. *de mensen hadden hard om de clown gelachen*

intransitive + passive
1. *er wordt gelachen*
2. *er werd gelachen*
3. *er is gelachen*
4. *er was gelachen*

intransitive + active
1. *hij blijft niet thuis*
2. *hij bleef niet thuis*
3. *hij is niet thuis gebleven*
4. *hij was niet thuis gebleven*

intransitive + active
1. *Els gaat naar een tentoonstelling*
2. *Els ging naar een tentoonstelling*
3. *Els is naar een tentoonstelling gegaan*
4. *Els was naar een tentoonstelling gegaan*

intransitive +active

1. *meneer Bergsma is   dood/meneer Bergsma is   gestorven*
2. *meneer Bergsma was dood/meneer Bergsma was gestorven*

intransitive + active

1. *de bibliotheek is   zondags gesloten/dicht*
2. *de bibliotheek was zondags gesloten/dicht*

transitive + passive

1. *de deur wordt 's avonds om tien uur precies gesloten*
2. *de deur werd 's avonds om tien uur precies gesloten*
3. *de deur is   's avonds om tien uur precies gesloten*
4. *de deur was   's avonds om tien uur precies gesloten*

APPENDIX C   WORD ORDER AND NEGATION

C1. THE PLACE OF THE VERB

1   THE PLACE OF THE VERB IN SIMPLE SENTENCES
1.1   In a simple sentence the PV comes in second position, even if the subject is not in initial position:

ik   geef het boek vanavond aan mijn vriend
vanavond   geef ik het boek aan mijn vriend
het boek   geef ik vanavond aan mijn vriend
aan mijn vriend geef ik vanavond het boek

1.2   If the verb consists of more than one word, e.g. Auxiliary (AUX) and Past Participle (PP) or AUX and Infinitive (INF), AUX comes in second position and the rest of the verb at the end of the sentence.

AUX + INF:
ik   zal het boek vanavond aan mijn vriend geven
vanavond   zal ik het boek aan mijn vriend   geven
het boek   zal ik vanavond aan mijn vriend   geven
aan mijn vriend zal ik vanavond het boek   geven

AUX + PP:
ik   heb het boek gisteren aan mijn vriend gegeven
gisteren   heb ik het boek aan mijn vriend   gegeven
het boek   heb ik gisteren aan mijn vriend   gegeven
aan mijn vriend heb ik gisteren het boek   gegeven

1.3   There are a number of exceptions to the rule that INF and PP come at the end of the sentence. The two of most importance are:

a) Most of the Prepositional Constituents (PREP-C) may follow INF or PP:

*ik zal het boek vanavond aan mijn vriend **geven***
*ik zal het boek vanavond **geven** aan mijn vriend*

*ik heb in Utrecht **gewoond***
*ik heb **gewoond** in Utrecht*

*ik heb gisteren naar het TV-journaal **gekeken***
*ik heb gisteren **gekeken** naar het TV-journaal*

*ik ben om drie uur **weggegaan***
*ik ben **weggegaan** om drie uur*

b) A subordinate clause must follow INF or PP:

ik heb hem gisteren	*gezegd*	***dat ik niet kom***
ik heb haar vorige week woensdag	*gevraagd*	***waar ze woont***
ik kan nu geen boodschappen	*doen*	***omdat ik op een telefoontje wacht***

2 THE PLACE OF THE VERB IN COMPOUND SENTENCES

2.1 A compound sentence consists of at least one main clause and one subclause. In the subclause the verb is at the end. If the verb consists of AUX and INF or of AUX and PP, then these occur together at the end; the order is not important: AUX + PP or PP + AUX, and AUX + INF or INF + AUX are equally possible.

ik blijf vanavond thuis,	*omdat ik om ongeveer 8 uur bezoek*	***krijg***
ik ga met je mee,	*als het vanmiddag tenminste niet zo hard*	***gaat regenen*** ***regenen gaat***
ik blijf vandaag thuis,	*omdat ik drie weken lang erg ziek*	***ben geweest*** ***geweest ben***

2.2 If the subclause comes before the main clause, the PV of the main clause follows immediately after the subclause. This is because the complete subclause is seen as comprising the first constituent of the sentence:

omdat ik om ongeveer 8 uur bezoek krijg,	***blijf***	*ik vanavond thuis*
als het vanmiddag niet gaat regenen,	***ga***	*ik met je mee*
als het vanmiddag niet regenen gaat,	***ga***	*ik met je mee*
omdat ik ziek ben geweest,	***blijf***	*ik thuis*
omdat ik ziek geweest ben,	***blijf***	*ik thuis*
omdat ik bezoek krijg,	***heb***	*ik een fles champagne gekocht*
omdat ik bezoek krijg,	***ga***	*ik een fles champagne kopen*

2.3 The exceptions mentioned in 1.3 are also applicable here. So a PREP-C may optionally follow the verb and if there is another subclause then this must follow the verb:

ik blijf thuis omdat ik vanavond bezoek krijg	***van een vriend***
ik blijf thuis omdat jij gisteren tegen mij :*hebt gezegd,* *gezegd hebt,*	***dat het vandaag*** ***gaat regenen*** ***regenen gaat***

C2. NEGATION WITH *GEEN* AND *NIET*

1 GEEN
1.1 Sentence negation with **geen**

Geen is a combination of **negation + indefinite article.**
Examples:

ik heb geen televisie
ik heb geen boeken
ik heb geen mooi huis
ik heb helemaal geen schoenen
ik heb geen koffie meer
ik drink geen bier
ik studeer geen economie
ik ben geen student
ik ben geen Engelsman
ik heet geen Peter
ik heb gehoord dat je geen televisie hebt
ik hoor dat je geen huis wilt kopen
ik hoor dat je geen Nederlander bent
ik hoor dat je geen alcohol wilt drinken
ik hoor dat je nog geen pannekoeken hebt gegeten

1.2 Phrase negation with **geen**
An indefinite noun phrase (NP) is mostly made negative with **geen**.
Examples:

ik heb geen TV maar wel een radio
hij drinkt geen bier maar wijn
zij studeert geen economie maar sociologie
zij is geen Engelse maar Française
hij heet geen Peter maar Wim

2 NIET
2.1 Sentence negation with **niet**
2.1.1 Since the verb in a subclause occurs mostly at the end of the clause (see appendix C1), **niet** in a subclause immediately precedes the verb. In a main clause, however, the PV is in second position (see lesson 2) and **niet** will normally follow the PV, but precede INF or PP. If present, **niet** also comes after a (definite) direct object and adjuncts such as *hier, daar, er, morgen, vanochtend* etc.

APPENDIX C

subclause	main clause
*hij zegt dat hij niet **rookt***	*hij **rookt** niet*
*hij zegt dat hij niet **gerookt heeft***	*hij heeft niet **gerookt***
*hij zegt dat hij niet **gaat studeren***	*hij gaat niet **studeren***
*hij zegt dat hij de boeken van Maria niet **heeft***	*hij heeft de boeken van Maria niet*
*hij zegt dat hij de jas van Kees niet **heeft gezien***	*hij heeft de jas van Kees niet gezien*
*hij zegt dat hij Nederlands niet **kan verstaan***	*hij kan Nederlands niet verstaan*
*hij zegt dat hij morgen niet **komt***	*hij komt morgen niet*
*hij zegt dat hij vanavond niet **kan komen***	*hij kan vanavond niet komen*
*hij zegt dat Kees er niet **is***	*Kees is er niet*
*hij zegt dat de bus hier niet **gestopt heeft***	*de bus heeft hier niet gestopt*
*hij zegt dat dat Wim niet **is***	*dat is Wim niet*
*hij zegt dat dat de trein naar Utrecht niet **is***	*dat is de trein naar Utrecht niet*

2.1.2 *Niet* is always said (both in main clause and in subclause) before:
1. a prepositional constituent
2. *beneden, boven, buiten, binnen, thuis*
3. an adjective (with the verbs *zijn, worden* and *blijven*)

subclause	main clause
*hij zegt dat hij niet **in** Utrecht studeert*	*hij studeert niet **in** Utrecht*
*hij zegt dat hij niet **in** Amsterdam gaat wonen*	*hij gaat niet **in** Amsterdam wonen*
*hij zegt dat hij niet **om** 4 uur thuis komt*	*hij komt niet **om** 4 uur thuis*
*hij zegt dat de kinderen niet **thuis** zijn*	*de kinderen zijn niet **thuis***
*hij zegt dat het huis niet **groot** is*	*het huis is niet **groot***
*hij zegt dat de problemen niet **ernstig** zullen zijn*	*de problemen zullen niet **ernstig** zijn*

2.2   The negation of a single constituent with *niet*
Niet immediately precedes the constituent in question (but the PV of the main clause takes up second position):

subclause	main clause
*hij zegt dat hij niet **morgen** maar vandaag zal komen*	*hij zal niet **morgen** maar vandaag komen*
*hij zegt dat dat niet **Wim** maar Kees is*	*dat is niet **Wim** maar Kees*
*hij zegt dat hij niet **de auto** maar wel de fiets van Kees geleend heeft*	*hij heeft niet **de auto** maar wel de fiets van Kees geleend*
*hij zegt dat de stoel niet **hier** bij de deur maar daar bij het raam moet staan*	*de stoel moet niet **hier** bij de deur maar daar bij het raam staan*
*hij zegt dat hij wel rookt maar niet **drinkt***	*hij rookt wel maar hij **drinkt** niet*
*hij zegt dat hij niet **gaat slapen** maar wel gaat werken*	*hij **gaat** niet **slapen** maar wel werken*
*hij zegt dat hij het ei niet **gekookt** maar gebakken heeft*	*hij heeft het ei niet **gekookt** maar gebakken*
*hij zegt dat hij het ei niet **kookt** maar bakt*	*hij **kookt** het ei niet maar bakt het*
*hij zegt dat het niet **regent** maar sneeuwt*	*het **regent** niet maar het sneeuwt*

APPENDIX D   PRONOUNS

D1. A SUMMARY OF THE USES OF *DIE* AND *DAT*

1 As demonstratives in the sense of 'over there':

dat gebouw (daar aan de overkant van de straat) is een postkantoor
deze boeken hier zijn van mij, maar die boeken (daar in die boekenkast naast het raam) zijn
van mijn vader
is dit úw fiets? nee, deze niet, maar die wel: daar onder die boom daar
wat is dat daar in de verte?

2 *Die/dat* contrast wich *deze/dit* when two objects or persons are equidistant from the speaker:

heb je even een pen voor me?
ja natuurlijk. welke wil je: deze of die?

we hebben twee soorten overhemden
kijk, dit overhemd kost f 17,90 en dat overhemd kost f 29,95

kijk, dit is een dubbeltje en dat is een kwartje

3 'First reaction to a new topic' (see lesson 8 and Appendix D2):

ken je Anneke van Kampen?
nee, die ken ik niet

weet je waar Anneke is?
nee, dat weet ik niet

weet jij soms waar de melk is?
die staat in de koelkast

ken jij Anneke van Kampen?
eh, is dat niet de vriendin van Kees Bergsma?

4 *Die/dat* = 'that which is familiar'; the speaker assumes that the thing(s) or the person(s) he is talking about is (are) already known to the hearer:

zeg Anneke, heb jij die nieuwe Japanse film al gezien? (lesson 13, line 1)
je gaat vanavond uit, hè? Doe je die rode jurk aan? (lesson 15, line 5)
ik kan dat mooie zakdoekje niet vinden, dat witte met die bloemetjes (lesson 15, line 22-23)

5 *Die van . . . , dat van . . . ,* as constructions that express possession:

Anneke, mag ik je fiets misschien lenen? die van mij heeft geen licht. neem die van Wim maar (lesson 15, line 60)
je hebt toch zelf een tasje, waarom pak je dat van mij dan? (lesson 15, line 15-16)

6 *Die* and *dat* as relatives (in initial position in a relative clause):

hier is de kamer die ik voor u heb
het bureau dat ik heb, is van hout
het boek dat daar op tafel ligt, is niet van mij
de boeken die daar staan, zijn van jou nietwaar?

7 *Dat* (not *die*)as a conjunction:

Kees zegt dat John ziek is
ik geloof niet dat het gaat regenen
het is jammer dat je nu al weg moet

N.B. *dag mevrouw, die kamer die u te huur hebt, is die nog vrij?* (lesson 8 (line 3))

> The three examples of *die* in this sentence occur in the functions of 4, 6 and 3 respectively.

D2. THE USE OF *DIE, DAT* AND *DAAR* (+ PREPOSITION) AS ALTERNATIVES TO THE PRONOMINAL FORMS *HIJ/HEM, ZE/HAAR, HET, ER*

There are two different ways of referring pronominally to a person or thing. For instance, if you want to refer to *de fiets van Anneke* you may use either *die* or *hij* in subject function, e.g.
die is kapot
hij is kapot
The problem is when to use *die* and when *hij*. Generally speaking if someone or something is mentioned in a conversation for the first time, then we can speak of a new '(discourse) topic'. If subsequently something is said about this topic, then this **'initial reaction'** will usually refer to it by means of *die/dat/daar*. In declarative sentences these words tend to take up initial position, even when they do not function as subject. The function of *die, dat* and *daar* can then be characterised as a 'first reaction to a new topic'.
The standard pronouns *hij, hem, ze, haar, het, er* are usually used when the referent re-occurs later on in the discourse, in other words in sentences which one might label as a 'second or later reaction to a (new) topic'.
The table below gives a survey of the use of *die* and *dat* as alternatives to the standard pronouns:

1. *personen*	subject		object	
Els	ze	die	haar	die
Kees	hij	die	hem	die
Kees en Els	ze	die	ze	die

2. *zaken*				
de jas	hij	die	hem	die
de jassen	ze	die	ze	die
het boek	het	dat	het	dat
de boeken	ze	die	ze	die

Note also that *daar* can replace both *er₁* and *er₄* (see appendix D3):

Kees woont in Zwolle	*Kees woont **er***	*Kees woont **daar***
Kees houdt van whisky	*Kees houdt **ervan***	*Kees houdt **daarvan***

Here are some examples of the use of the various pronouns in discourse:

*is Els ziek? nee, **die** is niet ziek. ik heb **haar** daarnet nog gezien. **ze** zit in de leeszaal*

*ken je Els en Jaap niet? **die** wonen op het Olympiaplein, weet je wel. je hebt **ze** toch op de receptie gezien? **ze** werken allebei in een ziekenhuis*

*opera? nee hoor, **daar** houd ik niet van. mijn vrouw wel. **die** houdt **er** wel van*

*waar is je dictaat? **dat** heb ik niet bij me. wil je **het** soms van me lenen? maar **het** is niet erg netjes, hoor!*

*ben je wel eens in Zwolle geweest? nee, **daar** daar ben ik nog nooit geweest. maar mijn broer komt **er** vaak, want **die** moet **er** vaak zijn voor zijn werk*

*mevrouw van Mierlo? ja, **dat** is een kennis van me, of liever: **het** is een kennis van mijn moeder*

D3. THE FUNCTIONS OF *ER*

The most important functions of *er* are:

1 *Er* as a locational adverbial. *Er* is equivalent to the locative adverb 'there' in English:

*ik ben naar Utrecht verhuisd. ik woon **er** nu al weer twee maanden*
*ik heb wel een leuke kamer, maar ik heb **er** geen zon*

2 Introductory *er* with an indefinite subject:

*maar vader, **er** is geen melk en **er** zijn geen eieren!*
***er** staat een rode auto voor de deur*
***er** zijn twee telefooncellen in deze straat, maar **er** is geeneen brievenbus*

3 *Er* combined with **(g)een, twee, drie, vier, vijf, weinig, veel, genoeg,** etc.:

*heb jij nog kaartjes? ja, ik heb **er** nog drie. wil jij **er** een hebben? heb jij **er** geeneen meer?*

4 *Er* combined with a preposition instead of an impersonal object:

*ik houd **er** niet **van** (van opera's)*
*ik kijk **er** nooit **naar** (naar motorraces)*
*hij praat **er** wel eens met me **over** (over die moeilijkheden)*
*hij gaat **er** nooit **naartoe** (naar de cursus Nederlands)*
*hij komt **er** net **vandaan** (van het postkantoor)*

N.B.₁ *Er* is never said twice in succession:
>*hoeveel flessen staan **er** op tafel? **er** staan **er** vier op tafel. **er** staan **er** daar vier.*
>*er staan **er** vier. weet je dat zeker? liggen **er** niet vijf?*

>*hoeveel recensies staan **er** in de krant? **er** staan **er** drie vandaag (**er** staan **er** vandaag drie in de krant)*

>*hier in de straat komt geen tram, maar **er** stopt wel een bus* (combination of *er₁* and *er₂*)

N.B.₂ *Er₂* is said before the PV, if possible, and the indefinite subject after the PV.
N.B.₃ If possible, *er₃* and *er₄* follow directly after the PV.
N.B.₄ *Er₁* and *er₂* can never occur together in the same clause. In the following example *er* is thus to be seen as combining the locative and introductory meanings:

in die straat komt geen tram	there isn't a tram that comes along that street
*maar **er** stopt wel een bus*	but there is a bus that stops there

INDEX

Example: the entry **pronouns**

  relative 18.2.1; app. D1 means that relative pronouns are dealt with in lesson 18, section 2.1 and in Appendix D1.

INDEX

INDEX

INDEX